Chemically Active!

Also by Vicki Cobb

Fuzz Does It!
Gobs of Goo
How to Really *Fool Yourself*
Lots of Rot
Magic... Naturally! Science Experiments and Amusements
More Science Experiments You Can Eat
Science Experiments You Can Eat
The Secret Life of Hardware: A Science Experiment Book
The Secret Life of School Supplies
Supersuits

Vicki Cobb

Chemically Active!

Experiments You Can Do at Home

Illustrated by
Theo Cobb

J.B. Lippincott   New York

For F.S.T., friend

The author gratefully acknowledges the technical advice and expertise of chemist Dr. Bruce Deck, of the Lamont-Doherty Geological Observatory of Columbia University, and the laboratory assistance of his young friends Maureen Guilfoyle, Jennifer Long, and Michael Schneider.

Chart on page 116 reproduced from The Merck Index Tenth Edition 1983, published by Merck & Co., Inc., Rahway, New Jersey.

Library of Congress Cataloging in Publication Data
Cobb, Vicki.
    Chemically active!

    Summary: Gives instructions for performing a variety
of experiments, using easily available materials, that
illustrate some basic principles of chemistry.
    1. Chemistry—Experiments—Juvenile literature.
[1. Chemistry—Experiments.   2. Experiments]   I. Cobb,
Theo, ill.   II. Title.
QD38.C63   1985   540'.7'8   83-49490
ISBN 0-397-32079-5
ISBN 0-397-32080-9 (lib. bdg.)

Designed by Barbara A. Fitzsimmons
10 9 8 7 6 5 4 3 2 1
First Edition

CONTENTS

Chemically Active!

A Word Before You Begin

Chemistry is the science that deals with matter and the ways matter changes. Chemistry suggests mental pictures of conjuring, of beakers and bottles and smelly substances and of heating and distilling, mixing and separating. Chemistry also has a reputation of being difficult to understand, a subject you need a special talent for. Not so! Chemistry can be for anyone. It is the purpose of this book to present the principles of this fascinating science so that you can share the fascination and experience its magic. Naturally, you will do experiments. Chemistry is primarily a laboratory science, and no appreciation is possible unless you do your own conjuring and make systematic changes in substances you have around the house. So before you begin, let me give you some suggestions about how to use this book.

You can, first of all, simply read this book from cover

to cover, as you would any book of nonfiction. Chemistry is explained here in a logical fashion, chapter by chapter, each topic building on the ideas introduced earlier. First you'll discover the nature of matter, then the nature of chemical reactions. Next you'll investigate some of the more common forms of matter and begin to explore the electrical aspects of matter. By this time, you should have discovered enough about chemistry through experience to feel the need for some sense to be made out of it; now you are ready to learn about the theories underlying the science. These are presented and explained in chapter 6. The last two chapters present chemical procedures applied to research questions and to some sophisticated stunts.

The important ideas in each chapter are illustrated with experiments, the heart of a science like chemistry. So the best way to use this book is to do the experiments in the order in which they occur as you read through the book.

When you do an experiment, read through the procedure before you start. Collect everything you need before you begin so that you're not caught short looking for something at a crucial moment in a procedure. The procedure is the way a scientist goes about getting information. Good procedures give clear-cut results. The procedures in this book have all been tested in my home laboratory, and they work.

A FEW WORDS OF WARNING.

Many of the procedures involve using the stove, or a flame. Many involve substances that are poisonous or that may be highly inflammable or harmful to your skin or eyes or clothes. Wash your hands carefully after using them. Some substances produce irritating fumes. They should be used in well-ventilated areas. CHECK WITH AN ADULT BEFORE YOU BEGIN ANY EXPERIMENT. Read all labels and respect warnings and follow the experiment directions carefully. Don't mix household chemicals unless you understand the dangers and have an adult present. If you follow these rules, you will not be in danger. As a reminder watch for these symbols: ◊ ✗ ﹖ ▲ which will appear in the Materials and Equipment section of the experiments.

◊ FLAME

✗ POISON

﹖ FUMES

▲ DAMAGE TO SKIN OR CLOTHES

Make sure you use clean glassware in your experiments. When you wash up, rinse all the soap from the glassware and let it dry. Glass is clean because water drains off without leaving drops behind. Cleanliness is important in chemistry because unknown substances left behind on your glassware or measuring instruments can sometimes confuse results.

End of lecture. Now it's time for you to get your mind and hands into matter, to discover what it's like and what you can do with it. Experiment with chemistry, just for the fun of it!

1. Mysterious Concoctions

Want to make some strange things happen in a bowl? You can cook up a purple liquid that has weird and mysterious powers. Add a pinch of white powder, and it turns pink. Another pinch of something else turns it green. Put in a few drops of a clear liquid, and the concoction turns pink while developing a humungous foaming head. There's almost no end to the changes you can make in this solution that turns colors and blows bubbles.

Here's another. Want to collect something you can't see or feel or smell, but that sits in a jar without a cover? No one can tell it's there. Yet when you hold it over a candle flame and make a pouring motion, the flame goes out. Instantly!

Magic? No. Chemistry. Do these things and you'll look and feel like a mad chemist. I'm betting that this kind of fun will make you want to know more about what's really happening in the bowl or jar. You'll want to understand the science behind the magic. Understanding science, *doing* science, is even more fun than just making mysterious things happen.

So, in this chapter, I'm going to give you instructions for some experiments that will make you open your eyes in surprise. They will fire your imagination. Watch the action. Introduce yourself to chemistry—the science of matter and the ways it changes. Discover for yourself a science in which truth is more magical than the magic of mysterious concoctions. Get ready. You are about to have an adventure!

Essence of Cabbage

The key ingredient of this concoction is the red material in red cabbage. Your first problem is to get the red out. You will then have the essential stuff for lots of chemical action.

MATERIALS AND EQUIPMENT
    1 small red cabbage
    grater
    stainless steel or enamel (not aluminum) saucepan
    water

strainer
mixing bowl
measuring cup
large mayonnaise jar
teaspoon
white vinegar
soap flakes (not detergent)
cream of tartar
baking soda
▲ ✗ chlorine bleach (CAUTION!)

Ingredients for "Essense of Cabbage" experiment.

PROCEDURE

Grate about two cups of cabbage into the saucepan. Cover it with water. CHECK WITH AN ADULT BEFORE YOU USE THE STOVE FOR THE NEXT STEP. Heat the cabbage and water until the water boils. Notice that the red in the cabbage is now mostly in the water. Collect the red cabbage water by pouring the mixture through the strainer set over the bowl.

Now for the fun part. Put about a cup of the red cabbage water into the jar. It should be between ⅓ and ½ full. Stir in about a teaspoon of each of the other ingredients — the white vinegar, the soap flakes, the cream of tartar, one by one. Some things will turn the red juice green. Some things will turn it pink. Sooner or later your concoction will foam up and possibly overflow its container, so do your adding over the sink. If you feel you've gone as far as you wish with your first sample, pour it out and start again. Be sure to wash out all glassware well between experiments.

OBSERVATIONS AND SUGGESTIONS

To sharpen your chemist's eye, here are a few things to look for: Which items turn the juice green? Which turn the green juice pink? Which two items on the list do you need to mix together to get foam? Check your hunch by mixing them in water instead of cabbage juice. Is the cabbage juice needed for this reaction?

To take your discoveries one step further, here are some other experiments you might try: Try the essence of other red fruits and vegetables. Make extracts of fresh beets, cherries, blueberries, violets or irises by chopping up small quantities of them and boiling them in water the same way you made the extract of the cabbage juice. Use them the same way you used the cabbage juice, as the basis for your experiments. Be sure to keep a written record of the things you try and your results. Keep any unused cabbage juice and other extracts in the refrigerator. Like any food product, these juices can spoil so throw them out if they start to smell bad.

If you're wondering about what you've just done, good! You will find out what happens as you learn about acids, bases, chemical indicators and chemical reactions later on in this book.

Extract of Soda Pop

In this experiment you are going to collect the stuff that makes the bubbles in soda pop. To do this, you have to make some apparatus. But you'll be able to use the same apparatus for other experiments, too, so it's well worth the trouble.

12-inch length of plastic tubing from an aquarium store

plastic clay (Plasticine)

unopened bottle of soda pop

large washbasin ⅔ full of water

several small jars (jelly jars, for example)

plastic disks for each small jar (such as plastic covers from coffee or tennis ball cans)

small bowl of hot tap water

♦ kitchen matches

birthday cake candles in holders (See p. 14)

PROCEDURE

The plastic tubing is going to transfer the gas from the soda pop into the small jars. To make your delivery system, pinch off a wad of clay and stick one end of the tubing through it. Open the bottle of soda and mold the wad of clay into an airtight stopper by pushing it into the mouth of the bottle. Put the other end of the tubing in the large basin of water. Do you see bubbles coming out of the tubing? Don't worry if you don't.

Submerge one of the small jars in the basin, completely filling it with water. Turn the jar upside down and rest it on the bottom of the basin until you're ready. There should be no air pocket in the jar.

To drive off the gas in the soda, stand the soda bottle in the small bowl of hot tap water. Watch the end of your

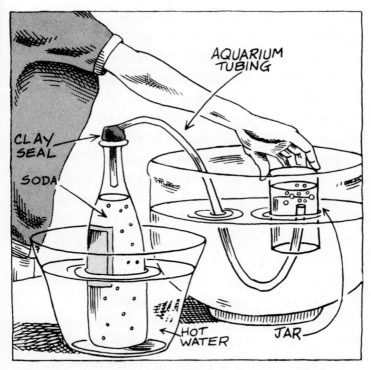

Collection of carbon dioxide by the displacement of water.

delivery tube in the basin. Bubbles should start coming from the tube. Hold the inverted, water-filled collecting jar in the basin over the delivery tube as shown in the picture. The bubbles will rise to the surface and drive out the water from the jar back into the basin. This method of collecting a gas is called *displacement of water*. When you have completely filled the jar with gas, bubbles will form in the water outside the jar and rise to the surface. Still holding the gas-filled jar upside down and under water, remove the delivery tube from the jar, leaving the tube in the basin, and slide a plastic disk across the mouth of the jar. (Be careful not to tilt the jar, or water will rush in, driving out your precious gas.) Hold the disk in place as you remove the inverted jar from the water. Turn the jar right side up when you have removed it from the basin. Set it aside with the lid on. Collect more jars of gas until there is no more fizz coming from the soda.

OBSERVATIONS AND SUGGESTIONS

Remove the plastic lid from one of the jars of gas. Let the jar sit undisturbed for a few minutes, open to the air, while you do the next experiments.

FIRST CHECK WITH AN ADULT BEFORE USING MATCHES. Remove the top from a second jar. Strike a match and lower it into the jar. Extract of soda puts out the flame!

Light a candle and make a pouring motion over it with the jar of gas you just used to put out the match. Again, the fire is doused.

You have discovered two important things about the gas in the jar: it puts out a flame and it is heavier than air. (That's the reason you can pour it. If it were lighter than air, it would escape up into the air if left to stand in an open jar.) So check this out. The gas should still be in the first jar you left standing open. Experiment to see if this is so. Use the gas in the first jar to repeat the tests with the match and the candle. Usually this heavier-than-air gas will stay put for about half an hour before spilling up into the air. If your room is drafty, however, the gas may empty more quickly. Check this out for yourself.

Here's still another fun thing to do. Make a wire candle holder with a pipe cleaner or some picture-hanging wire

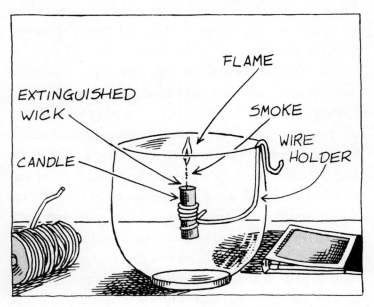

A flame burns only where there's oxygen.

and wrap it around a candle, as shown in the picture (previous page). Make sure the candle is held securely in a vertical position. Lower a lit candle into one of the jars of soda pop gas. If you keep the candle perfectly vertical, the flame stays at the mouth of the jar, separated from the wick beneath it. A thin column of smoke trails from the wick to the invisible surface of the gas where the burning is taking place. You've separated the flame from its wick! The gas in the jar extinguishes the flame, but a stream of hot wax rises like smoke from the wick. When it reaches the surface of the gas in the jar (which you can't see, of course), the hot wax burns because it is in the air.

This mysterious extract of soda, which you may know as *carbon dioxide*, was once called "the gas sylvester." "Sylvester" comes from a Latin word meaning "woods" or "forest" because the gas was found in caves containing rotting wood. The gas sylvester formed a layer on the floor of caves and stayed close to the ground. There was no wind to blow it away so it remained in place. There are stories of dogs that died when they went into such caves. They suffocated to death because they breathed this heavy gas that had displaced the needed air. It was a mysterious death because a person accompanying the dog would not be harmed. The human head was above the surface of the carbon dioxide.

2. What's the Matter with Matter?

Matter is the stuff and substance of the universe. It is wood and steel; it is water, earth and air. There is living matter, such as animals and plants; nonliving matter, such as salt and plastic; and dead matter, such as food and last year's leaves. Matter, to a scientist, is anything that takes up space and has weight (more precisely known as *mass*). The nature of matter is the subject of chemistry.

So you, a budding chemist, can look at matter all around you and easily see what's the matter with matter. It comes in a great variety of forms. Matter is complicated. Most of the matter you see is a mixture of several kinds of materials. Some matter is hard, some is soft. Some can be hammered into thin sheets, other kinds of matter will shatter if you hammer them. Matter can be of any color. It can be transparent or opaque. Some matter you can't see, although you may feel it and breathe it. There appears to be no end to the ways in which matter exists in the world. So the first order of the business of chemistry is to simplify matter: to break down materials into their basic components — to *analyze* matter by finding ways of detecting its basic components, and to discover the kinds of matter that cannot be broken down into anything simpler.

As you might expect, there are lots of ways to analyze matter. Some of these methods you are going to learn here. Analytical methods take advantage of different properties of matter. For example, some kinds of matter dissolve in water, others do not. Suppose you have a mixture that contains some water-soluble material and some insoluble material. You put the entire substance in water and then separate the soluble part with a filter. A filter is like a strainer but with much smaller holes. The next experiment requires some filtering; it will give you practice in this important procedure.

Preparing Iron Sulfate Solution

Professional chemists keep containers of pure chemicals, called *reagents* (ree-ay-jents), on their shelves. Reagents are used in many lab tests to identify unknown substances. Since reagents are known substances, chemists can discover unknown substances by comparing them with their reagents. As you begin your personal adventure into chemistry, start your own reagent shelf. Get some small jars with covers. Get some adhesive labels so that each of your reagents can be clearly marked. Be sure and close tightly all your reagent jars after each use.

Iron sulfate (also called *ferrous sulfate*) is a source of iron for the body. Iron is used to carry oxygen in your blood. You can make a solution of iron sulfate from tablets you can get at your local pharmacy.

MATERIALS AND EQUIPMENT
>5 iron sulfate tablets from any drugstore
>measuring cup
>spoon for stirring
>one folded circular coffee filter, or a circle of paper
>>toweling folded in quarters (see picture)
>funnel
>small jar for storing your solution
>label marked IRON SULFATE SOLUTION

PROCEDURE
Put the tablets in the measuring cup. Cover with about ½ cup of water. Stir. Notice that the dark outer coating of the tablet comes off and stains the water. Soak the tablets until the coating is completely dissolved. Rinse off

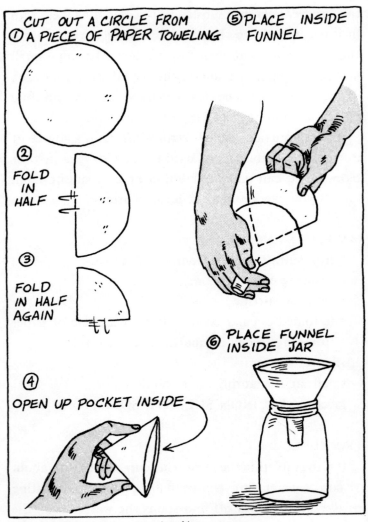

CUT OUT A CIRCLE FROM
① A PIECE OF PAPER TOWELING

⑤ PLACE INSIDE FUNNEL

② FOLD IN HALF

③ FOLD IN HALF AGAIN

④ OPEN UP POCKET INSIDE

⑥ PLACE FUNNEL INSIDE JAR

How to fold and insert the filter paper.

the tablets under the faucet. They should be white. Rinse out the cup, fill it with about ¾ cup warm water, and put the tablets in the cup. Stir until the tablets break up. The white powdery material that does not dissolve is a neutral material used by pharmaceutical firms in the manufacturing of the tablets.

To collect your iron sulfate solution and separate it from the white powder, filter the mixture. Open the coffee filter or circle of paper toweling to form a cone and put it in the funnel. Set the funnel in the jar. Stir the mixture well, then pour it into the filter. The material that passes through the filter is called the *filtrate*. The material trapped by the filter is called the *residue*. Let the filtrate drain into the jar. Cover the jar and label it.

OBSERVATIONS

The iron sulfate that is in the solution passes through the filter paper for the simple reason that the smallest units of iron sulfate and the smallest units of water are much smaller than the holes in the filter paper. The particles of white material are too large to pass through the tiny holes in the filter. Chemists use filters with different-sized holes (most of them so small than you cannot see them with an ordinary microscope). The size of the hole can be used to tell the size of the particles. If a substance shows up in the filtrate, its particles are smaller than the holes in the filter. If the substance remains in the residue, its particles are larger than the holes.

The original mixture—the tablets dissolved in warm water—that you filtered is called a *suspension* because some of the material, the neutral component, was suspended in the water. When you shake a suspension, it looks cloudy. True suspensions eventually settle if you allow them to stand long enough, and you can then separate the components by pouring off the solution that remains on top. The residue remains on the bottom. Filtering is a faster way of separating a filtrate from its residue.

Save your iron sulfate solution for the "iron test" experiment in chapter 3.

About Solutions

Solutions are a special kind of mixture. They are always evenly mixed, or *homogeneous*. Think of a solution as a mixture of at least two kinds of particles that are too small to see, with the particles evenly spread throughout the solution. You can test a sugar-water solution to prove to yourself that the sugar is evenly distributed. Stir about a teaspoon of sugar into a glass of warm water. Wait about five minutes before your test to make sure that the sugar is thoroughly dissolved. Using a clean straw, take a sip from the bottom and another from the top; the sip from the bottom should be just as sweet as the sip from the top. To get your samples of solution, cover the top of the straw with your finger and insert it in the solution, then raise your finger just enough to allow a small amount of solution to slip into the straw. Remove the sample from the glass by keeping your finger over the top of the straw. See illustration on page 24.

Solutions are a good place to begin thinking about the structure of matter. A solution can be thought of as having two *phases*. One phase is made up of particles that are in contact with each other. This is the *continuous* phase and it is called the *solvent*. In water solutions, the water is the solvent. The other phase is made up of particles that are separated from each other. This phase is *discontinuous* and is called the *solute*. Solute particles are surrounded by solvent particles.

The particles that are the simplest single unit of a substance are called *molecules*. In a sugar-water solution, the sugar separates into molecules as it dissolves. Each sugar molecule is surrounded by water molecules. Chemists try to describe all the events they observe in terms of the behavior of molecules, and of the building blocks of molecules, *atoms*.

It is possible to recover a solute from a solution. One way is to simply let the solvent evaporate. The solute will

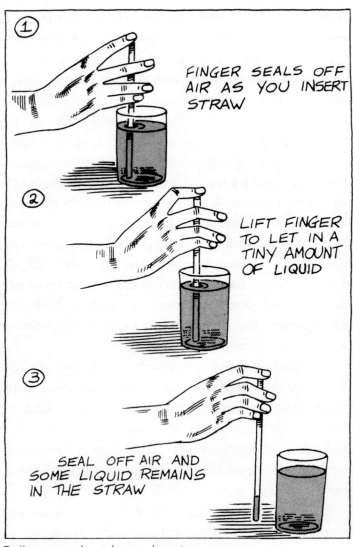

① FINGER SEALS OFF
AIR AS YOU INSERT
STRAW

② LIFT FINGER
TO LET IN A
TINY AMOUNT
OF LIQUID

③ SEAL OFF AIR AND
SOME LIQUID REMAINS
IN THE STRAW

Collecting a liquid sample using a straw.

be left behind. Of course, in that case you sacrifice the solvent. But if you want to separate a solute and solvent and recover the solvent, you can do this through a very clever procedure called *distillation*. See for yourself in the next experiment.

Distillation

Distillation takes advantage of another property of matter, namely, that a liquid can change into a gas. When you heat water, the molecules move faster and faster until they move so fast that they escape from the surface of the liquid. Steam is water in its gaseous form, escaping from the surface of boiling water. Molecules in a gas are separated from each other by relatively large distances. In a liquid, the molecules move around each other but they are in contact with each other. (We'll deal with the arrangement of molecules in solids in the next experiment.) You can change the state of a substance from a liquid to a gas by increasing the temperature. And you can change the state from a gas to a liquid by decreasing the temperature.

When you distill a solution, you boil the solvent, collect the gas, then cool the gas until it condenses back into a liquid in some other place. The solute often does not join the solvent molecules in the gaseous state. For this reason, chemists can use distillation to separate complicated mixtures.

25

MATERIALS AND EQUIPMENT

3-quart saucepan made of stainless steel, enamel or glass (not cast iron or aluminum)

stand for the collecting dish (such as a piece of brick or a small wide-mouthed jar filled with water and tightly closed)

small curved saucer or ashtray to be used as a collecting dish

measuring cup

teaspoon (optional)

water

food coloring

spices (optional) such as cloves, cinnamon, etc.

heat-resistant glass bowl (Pyrex), containing ice water, that fits over the saucepan

PROCEDURE

CHECK WITH AN ADULT BEFORE YOU USE THE STOVE. Put the saucepan on a stove burner. Put the piece of brick or the water-filled jar in the center of the saucepan and rest the collecting dish on it. Mix about 2 cups of cold water with a few drops of food coloring. You may also put in 3 teaspoons of some fragrant spice such as cinnamon or ground cloves. Pour the mixture into the saucepan. Be careful so that none of it accidentally lands in the collecting dish.

26

GLASS BOWL
FILLED WITH
ICE WATER

WATER
AND
SPICES

COLLECTING
DISH

MEDIUM HEAT

STAINLESS
STEEL
SAUCE-
PAN

Cutaway view of the distillation setup.

Cover the assemblage by placing over it the Pyrex or heat-resistant glass bowl containing ice water; then turn on a medium flame. (See the illustration.)

When the water in the saucepan boils, water vapor (steam) and some fragrant substances in the spices escape from the surface of the liquid to become gases. When these gases come in contact with the cold surface of the bowl, they condense into liquid water again and drop into the collecting dish. Distillation separates the solute molecules that "boil over" or travel with water from the ones that remain behind.

OBSERVATIONS AND SUGGESTIONS

If you added spices, smell the liquid in the collecting dish. Does it smell like the spice you used? Do food coloring molecules travel with water molecules?

Can you guess why distilled water is used for steam irons? To answer this question, let a dish of tap water evaporate completely (this may take several days) and check the material that remains behind.

You can use your distillation apparatus to make rose water. Put chopped petals of several roses in the pot with about two cups of water. Some of the fragrant substances in the petals will dissolve into the water. These molecules will boil over with the water molecules. Distill the fragrant rose water. You or your mother can use the distillate (which is left in the collecting cup) as perfume.

Crystallization

Another way to separate a solvent and a solute is to get the solute to form crystals. A crystal is an example of the third state of matter — a *solid*. A solid is a substance that has a definite shape and a definite volume. (In most cases, a liquid has a definite volume, but it takes the shape of its container, except at the surface. A gas has no definite shape and no definite volume. It takes both the shape and volume of its container.)

A crystal is also an example of *pure* stuff. A sample of pure stuff has only one kind of molecule throughout. The shape of a crystal is formed by the regular arrangement of its molecules. It also can be an indication of the shape of the molecule. Just as a stack of bricks neatly fitted together will take a shape determined by the shape of the bricks, so the final shape of a crystal is the result of the way its molecules fit together. The formation of a crystal lets a chemist know that he or she has a pure sample. A regular arrangement of molecules is not possible if molecules of different substances with different shapes are mixed together.

Here's the idea behind getting crystals to form from a solution. Crystal formation depends on the amount of solute dissolved in the solvent, which will be water in most of your experiments. The amount of solute you can dissolve in water depends on the solute and the temperature

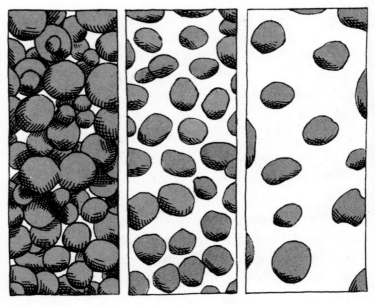

Molecules in a solid, liquid, and gas.

of the water. You can, for example, add sugar to cold water and stir. At some point the sugar will no longer dissolve and will just sit on the bottom of the mixture. At this point the water is holding as much sugar as it can and the solution is said to be *saturated*. Now suppose you heat the solution, moving the molecules faster. The extra solute dissolves. Add more sugar to the warm water until you can dissolve no more. And again you have a saturated solution. Since more sugar dissolves in warm water than in cold, the higher the temperature, the more sugar you need to make a saturated solution.

Now suppose you let a hot saturated solution cool. No crystals form, but you now have a solution holding more solute than would normally dissolve at that cooler temperature. Such a solution is called *supersaturated*. Another way you can get a supersaturated solution is to simply let the water evaporate. The solute becomes more concentrated as water leaves the solute behind. Under the right conditions, crystals form from a supersaturated solution. You will be growing crystals from both kinds of supersaturated solutions in the following experiments.

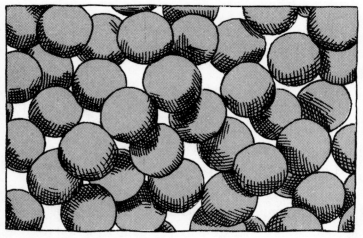

Molecules in a crystal.

Rock Candy Sugar Crystals

This is a popular activity because you can grow large sugar crystals that are good to eat. This is the only experiment in this book you can eat.

MATERIALS AND EQUIPMENT
  1/2 cup water
  1 cup granulated sugar
  measuring cup
  small saucepan
  wooden spoon
  jelly jar
  cotton string
  pencil
  small nut or paper clip to act as a weight

PROCEDURE

Make sure that all your equipment is clean. Put the water and sugar in the pan. Stir until you get as much of the sugar to dissolve as you can at that temperature. CHECK WITH AN ADULT BEFORE USING THE STOVE. Heat the mixture on a low flame, stirring constantly. Continue heating gently until all the sugar is dissolved. Bring the mixture to a boil and let it boil for one minute. Be careful not to let it burn.

Pour the hot syrupy solution into the jar. Hang a piece

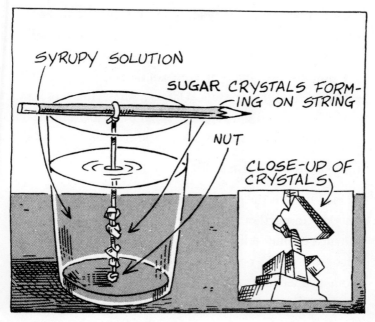

SYRUPY SOLUTION

SUGAR CRYSTALS FORM-
ING ON STRING

NUT

CLOSE-UP OF
CRYSTALS

Sugar crystals in rock candy.

of string, weighted down with a nut or a paper clip, into the solution. Hold the string in place by wrapping it around a pencil resting on top of the jar. Put the setup in a safe place and let stand.

OBSERVATIONS AND SUGGESTIONS

Let the solution stand undisturbed at room temperature. Check it every day and remove crystals that form on the surface so that the water can continue to evaporate. The crystals will form around any solid object. If you want to make rock-candy lollipops, put swizzle sticks into your solution. Be patient. Large crystals grow slowly. This will take days.

Compare the shape of your rock-candy crystals with granulated sugar crystals. Use a magnifying lens, and compare them to salt crystals. What do your findings tell you about the shapes of sugar and salt molecules?

Crystals on Glass

Jack Frost is the name given to the pattern of ice found on glass in northern winters. It forms as water vapor in the air becomes a liquid on the glass and then freezes to become a solid. You can make Jack Frost-like patterns from a supersaturated solution of Epsom salts (magnesium sulfate).

MATERIALS AND EQUIPMENT
measuring spoons
liquid detergent
measuring cup
small glass
paper towels (optional)
a flat, smooth transparent surface such as a piece of
    glass (take the glass out of a small picture frame)
    or some plastic wrap stretched taut over the mouth
    of a jar and held in place with a rubber band
magnesium sulfate (Epsom salts from any pharmacy)

PROCEDURE

Put ⅓ teaspoon of liquid detergent into a cup of water and stir. Put the glass in the sink or on paper towels and pour the soap solution over the surface so that it is completely flooded. Leave the glass lying flat and undisturbed while the soap solution dries. The thin film of soap that remains behind will make sure that your supersaturated solution spreads evenly over the surface.

Put 2 teaspoons magnesium sulfate in the small glass. CHECK WITH AN ADULT BEFORE USING THE STOVE. Stir in 1 tablespoon of boiling water. When all of the solute is dissolved, pour the magnesium sulfate solution over the dried surface of soap-filmed glass. Leave the glass flat in a safe place while you let the water evaporate. It may take up to an hour.

OBSERVATIONS AND SUGGESTIONS

Check your solution from time to time over the next hour. Watch as the crystals start to form on the glass. Where do they start forming first? Can you think why? How would you describe the shape of these crystals? Do they have the same shape as sugar crystals? As salt crystals? Use a magnifying lens to find out.

Magnesium sulfate crystals do something unusual with polarized light. Polarized light comes through one lens of Polaroid sunglasses. To see this effect, you need two lenses from a broken pair of Polaroid sunglasses.

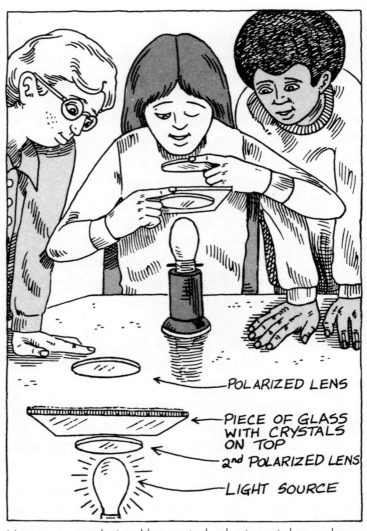

POLARIZED LENS

PIECE OF GLASS WITH CRYSTALS ON TOP

2nd POLARIZED LENS

LIGHT SOURCE

How to use polarized lenses to look at crystals on glass.

Here's how you can tell if your sunglass lenses are Polaroid lenses. Hold one lens over the other and look at a source of bright light. Slowly rotate one lens. If you have polaroid lenses, you will see that at some point most of the light is blocked. As you continue rotating the lens, it will get lighter and then darker again.

Crystals of magnesium sulfate also act like Polaroid lenses. Hold one lens below the glass on which you've grown your crystals. Hold both the lens and the glass over a light source while you look at the crystals through the other lens. Rotate the top lens until most of the light is blocked. You will see colors of the rainbow in your crystals.

If you are curious about this effect, read up on polarized light in a physical science book. This effect is a nice demonstration of the internal order of crystals. Not all crystals have this effect. You can use your lenses to look at other kinds of crystals you can grow on glass. (See the table on page 41.)

If you wish to grow magnesium sulfate crystals on a larger scale, you can grow structures like the ones you see in caves. Dissolve ⅔ cup of magnesium sulfate in 1 cup of boiling water. CHECK WITH AN ADULT BEFORE USING THE STOVE. Divide the supersaturated solution into two 4-ounce juice glasses. Put a paper clip on each end of a 12-inch length of unpolished cotton

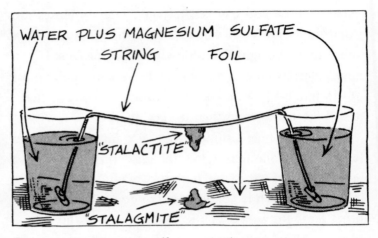

Growing magnesium sulfate crystals.

string. Wet the string thoroughly in the supersaturated solution and hang it between the glasses as shown. (Spread foil to protect your work surface.) Lo and behold a "stalactite" and "stalagmite" will grow over a period of several hours. A stalactite grows down and a stalagmite grows up. When they meet, they form a structure known as a "column."

Fast "Frozen" Crystals

The effect of this experiment is so spectacular that it is well worth the effort to find the reagent sodium thiosulfate, also known as hypo. You can get it at any well-stocked camera store, and a pound of it is quite inexpensive. The crystallization is reversible, so you can keep the solution around and repeat the procedure over and over again for the amusement of your friends.

MATERIALS AND EQUIPMENT
✗ sodium thiosulfate (hypo)
　measuring spoons
◊ boiling water
　heat-resistant custard cup
　asbestos pad
　spoon
　pot holder

PROCEDURE

Put 6 tablespoons of hypo into a custard cup. NOW, CHECK WITH AN ADULT BEFORE YOU USE THE STOVE. Add 2 tablespoons boiling water. Stir. Feel your solution. Notice how cold it gets. More on this later. Put the asbestos pad over a burner on the stove and turn on a low flame. Put the custard cup on the pad. Stir and heat the solution until it is perfectly clear and there is no evidence of any solute crystals. Turn off the heat and let the solution cool for fifteen minutes. Then put the mixture in the freezer to chill it well. Leave it there for twenty minutes to half an hour. (Do not let it freeze.) When you remove it, it should still be clear, without any sign of crystals. If there are some crystals in the solution, heat the mixture until they are gone and chill it again.

Drop 1 tiny sodium thiosulfate crystal into your solution. This crystal is called a *seed crystal*.

OBSERVATIONS AND SUGGESTIONS

As if by magic, crystals start growing from your seed. Within less than a minute the contents of the cup will be completely solid. Feel the cup. The increase in temperature is due to heat given off as the crystals form. This is called *heat of crystallization*. The same amount of heat is removed when crystals dissolve. That's why the custard cup became cold when you first mixed the hypo and boiling water. As the crystals dissolve (that is, become a solution), heat is removed from the water. During crystallization (the opposite process), heat is given off.

To repeat this effect, simply heat your solid crystals and repeat the procedure.

Other Crystals to Grow

There are other easy-to-get chemicals that you can use to grow crystals. Grow them on a glass plate to see if they show the polarized light effect. Compare the shapes of the crystals.

Here are the substances and the approximate amounts you need to get supersaturated solutions. You can make larger amounts by multiplying the proportions.

SUBSTANCE	AMOUNT OF SOLUTE	AMOUNT OF BOILING WATER
cream of tartar	1 tablespoon	2 ounces
table salt	2 tablespoons	2 ounces
washing soda (sodium carbonate)	4 tablespoons	3 ounces

Note: Some of the crystals will appear powdery after a while. This happens because the water that is in the structure of the crystals evaporates. Dehydrated powder is the result.

3. Magical Matter Transformations, Also Known as Chemical Reactions

Think of all the things we do with water in the course of an ordinary day. We wash ourselves and our clothes in it. We make ice cubes with it. We may crush the ice cubes before putting them in drinks. We use it to make tea and coffee and soup. We dissolve sugar and salt in it. We may heat our homes with it. But there is something most of us *don't* do with water. We don't change its basic nature. No matter how much we may freeze it, or boil it, or mix it with other things, water remains, pure and simply, water. Scientists call such a change of the form or state of a substance, one that does not change its composition, a *physical change*. Physical changes and their measurements, such as the temperatures at which a substance melts and boils, are useful for identifying substances.

A burning candle, on the other hand, is a totally different matter. You start out with wax and and a wick and, if you let the process go to completion, you end up with what appears to be nothing but the ash of the wick. Such a transformation, where you end up with something very different from what you started with, is called a *chemical change*. Chemical changes happen through events called *chemical reactions*. Chemists identify and describe different kinds of matter by their physical properties and by two kinds of chemical reactions. They are interested in the chemical reactions that produce different kinds of matter as well as the reactions matter enters into. It is through chemical reactions that we learn about the basic composition of matter.

In this chapter the experiments you do will help you discover some of the ways a chemist knows when a chemical reaction is taking place.

Energy Is Given Off

A flame is heat and light energy. Such an output of energy is a sure sign that a chemical reaction is taking place. Do the following experiments to analyze the chemical reaction of burning, called *combustion*.

MATERIALS AND EQUIPMENT

◊ large candle

  plastic clay or other device to hold
    candle in a basin of water

  pan of water

◊ kitchen matches

  jar large enough to fit over the candle and holder

  heat-resistant custard cup (Pyrex) or glass of ice water

  scissors

  aluminum foil

  pot holder

  old white china saucer (not plastic)

  plastic straw

  spoon

  pin

PROCEDURE AND OBSERVATIONS

Since you will be using fire, CHECK WITH AN
ADULT BEFORE YOU BEGIN. REMEMBER TO
KEEP YOUR HANDS, HAIR, AND CLOTHES AWAY
FROM THE FLAME.

Experiment 1: Set the candle upright in the pan. Use melted wax carefully dripped from the candle or plastic clay
to hold it in place. Fill the pan ⅔ full with water. Light
the candle. Put the jar upside down over the candle.
Watch.

FLAME BURNS INSIDE GLASS USING UP OXYGEN

WHEN THE FLAME GOES OUT THE WATER LEVEL GOES UP INSIDE GLASS.

Experiment #1

To make a flame you need the candle, the match and something in the air. When that substance in the air is used up, the candle goes out. The jar limits the amount of air available to the flame. The water rising in the jar after the candle goes out is replacing the substance in the air used up by the flame. Yes, you guessed it. It's oxygen.

Experiment 2: What substances does a flame produce? To discover one of them, hold a heat-resistant custard cup, or the dried bottom of a glass of ice water, over a burning candle for a second or two. (Since the water forms as a vapor, the cold bottom of the glass will cause more water vapor to condense on it than on a glass at room temperature. The iced glass removes heat more quickly

Experiment #2

Experiment #3

than a custard cup at room temperature.) Examine the inside of the cup or the bottom of the glass. Do you see moisture? Water is one of the products of combustion.

REMEMBER TO CHECK WITH AN ADULT BEFORE DOING THESE EXPERIMENTS.

Experiment 3: Discover the other product of combustion. Cut out a circle of aluminum foil about 8 inches in diameter. (You can trace around a paper plate.) Fold it in half, and in half again. Cut off the tip where all the folds meet. Open it to make a cone with the hole in the center. Hold your cone upside down over the flame. (Use a pot holder or metal tongs, since it may get quite warm.) Hold a burning kitchen match over the hole. The match should go out as this end product of combustion leaves the flame. Guess what! This end product is carbon dioxide, the very same gas you collected in chapter 1 as "Essence of Soda Pop." You know for sure that that gas doesn't support combustion.

Experiment 4: To have combustion, you need fuel (such as a candle), oxygen and a source of heat. What happens if you remove some of the heat? To do this, hold the back of an old white china saucer in the flame. The china absorbs some of the heat. Soot collects on the saucer. Soot

Experiment #4

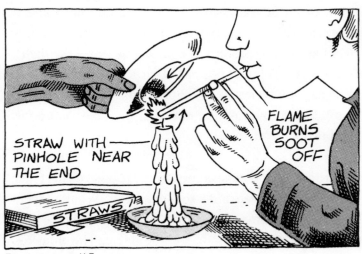

Experiment #5

is a substance called *carbon*. Carbon reacts chemically with oxygen in the air to make carbon dioxide. Remove some heat and there is not enough energy for carbon and oxygen to unite so carbon dioxide doesn't form. Carbon that is left in its uncombined state is the soot that collects on the saucer.

REMEMBER TO CHECK WITH AN ADULT BEFORE DOING THIS EXPERIMENT.

Experiment 5: Can you make carbon react with oxygen to form carbon dioxide if you increase the heat of the flame? If you increase the amount of oxygen you give to a flame, you also increase its heat. To demonstrate this, use a blowpipe made out of a straw. Put the end of a plastic straw in the flame for an instant until it melts but not long enough so that it burns. Press with a spoon against a counter top to squeeze the melted ends together to seal the straw. With a pin, make a small hole near the sealed end. Blow into the straw, with the hole pointed at the flame. You'll see that the flame gets bright yellow and is more focused. This is because you are adding more oxygen to the flame by blowing through the straw. Blow on the flame so that the hot yellow flame strikes a spot of soot on the saucer. (Be sure that your hair and clothes are not anywhere near the flame.) If you do it correctly, the spot will be burned clean. The oxygen will have combined with the carbon to make invisible carbon dioxide, which escapes into the air.

Some Additional Comments

Energy is involved in *all* chemical reactions. Some reactions, like combustion, give off energy. Combustion gives off so much energy that you have a flame of heat and light. Reactions, such as the "burning" of food in your body, give off less energy as heat and no light energy. Other reactions, like the making of sugar by green plants and the building of proteins in your body as it grows, require energy. Combustion needs an outside source of energy to get started. This energy is called the *kindling temperature.* Once the reaction gets started, however, it gives off enough energy to keep it going until the fuel or the oxygen is used up.

Firefighters need to remove either fuel, oxygen, or heat to stop a fire. Can you think of ways they do each of these things? Why does a wind "fan the flame"?

The overall principle of combustion can be stated as the following word equation:

$$\text{Fuel} + \text{oxygen} + \begin{array}{c} \text{(heat)} \\ \text{kindling} \\ \text{temperature} \end{array} \xrightarrow{\text{(yields)}} \text{water} + \text{carbon dioxide} + \text{energy}$$

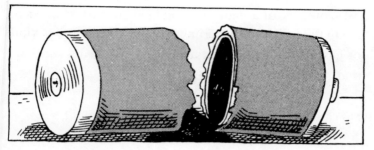

Manganese dioxide from a battery.

A Gas Is a Product

Chemical reactions occur as atoms and molecules encounter each other and form new combinations. In combustion, for example, carbon atoms and oxygen atoms combine to form molecules of carbon dioxide. In order for a chemical reaction to take place, molecules must come in contact with each other. This happens quite easily in solutions, so many of the reactions studied by chemists take place in a solution.

When a gas is a product of a chemical reaction in a solution, there can be no question a reaction is taking place. You see bubbles. The mixing of vinegar and baking soda, in the mysterious concoction you made in "Essence of Cabbage" in chapter 1, produces carbon dioxide. Mix some vinegar and baking soda in a jar. Hold a burning kitchen match over the bubbles near the surface. The extinguishing of a flame is a good test for carbon dioxide.

Do the following experiment to generate another kind of gas and to learn about a substance, called a *catalyst*, that speeds up a reaction.

MATERIALS AND EQUIPMENT

✗ hydrogen peroxide solution (from a drugstore)
  olive jars as alternative test tubes
✗ manganese dioxide *
  wooden toothpicks
  tongs
♦ matches
  very fresh hamburger meat or liver

PROCEDURE

Pour hydrogen peroxide into the jar until it is ⅓ full. Hold the jar up to the light. Do you see tiny bubbles forming and moving to the surface? Hydrogen peroxide is an unstable substance that, under normal conditions, breaks down slowly into oxygen and water.

Drop in a pinch of manganese dioxide. Stir or swirl the solution in the jar. Hold the end of a wooden tooth-

---

*An old flashlight battery is a good source of three things you need for experiments in this book. Carefully open an old D battery with a hammer and screwdriver. The black powder inside is mostly manganese dioxide, to be used in this experiment. Store it in a labeled jar. Scrape off the black carbon rod in the center of the battery. Save it for the experiment on page 61.

TOOTHPICK WITH GLOWING END

OOTHPICKS

HYDROGEN PEROXIDE + PINCH OF MANGANESE DIOXIDE

Oxygen makes a glowing toothpick flare up.

pick with metal tongs. Light the end of the toothpick. Let it flame up and then blow it out so the end is glowing. Put the glowing end of the toothpick into the jar. What effect does the gas have on the glowing toothpick?

OBSERVATIONS AND SUGGESTIONS

The flaming of the toothpick is a sure sign of the presence of oxygen, the gas that supports combustion. Put in a fresh sample of hydrogen peroxide. This time drop in a piece of fresh hamburger or liver. Again check the evolving gas to see if it is oxygen.

Manganese dioxide is a *catalyst* that speeds up the rate

at which the breakdown of hydrogen peroxide takes place. A catalyst doesn't become part of the reaction. It remains unchanged after the reaction is finished. Hydrogen peroxide will keep on giving off oxygen until there is no longer any left to react. But if you pour more hydrogen peroxide into the jar, the manganese dioxide has exactly the same power to catalyze the reaction in the fresh reagent — hydrogen peroxide — that it had originally.

Fresh meat and liver contain a catalyst called *catalase*, which also speeds up the breakdown of hydrogen peroxide. Catalase is an *enzyme*. All enzymes are catalysts for reactions that take place in living things. When you pour hydrogen peroxide on a cut, catalase in your blood causes the oxygen bubbles to froth up. Since many germs require an environment free of oxygen to grow, the oxygen generated by catalase acting on hydrogen peroxide acts as an antiseptic.

A Precipitate Forms

Another way to tell when a chemical reaction is taking place in a solution is if one of the products comes *out* of solution. Such an insoluble product is called a *precipitate*. Sometimes the precipitate has no color. But you can tell that it has formed because the solution suddenly becomes cloudy. At other times the precipitate may have a color that makes it easy to detect. In both cases, the formation of an insoluble substance tells the chemist that a new product has formed and a chemical reaction has taken place. Do the following experiments to see for yourself this kind of chemical reaction.

Iron Test

There are many substances that contain iron combined with other substances. When iron in solution comes in contact with tannic acid, a substance in tea, a precipitate of iron tannate forms.

MATERIALS AND EQUIPMENT

    2 cups of cooled strong tea (instant tea can be used)
    small juice glasses
    ferrous sulfate solution (saved from chapter 2)
    fruit juices, especially cranberry juice and pineapple
            juice
    steel wool (without soap — from a hardware store)
    vinegar
    leather

PROCEDURE

Pour the cooled tea into the juice glasses so they are about ½ full. Add the ferrous sulfate solution to one glass. DO NOT DRINK ANY SOLUTION. The black precipitate of iron tannate that forms was once used as ink. Can you write with your product? Dip in a crow quill pen (a metal nib in a holder) or a toothpick and try.

Test the fruit juices by putting about two tablespoons of juice in a sample of tea. Use a different glass of tea for each juice you test. Which fruit juices show the iron tannate precipitate when you add them to tea? If you wish to use iced tea as the basis of a fruit punch, which juices should you use to keep the tea clear?

Put some steel wool into one glass of tea. Does a precipitate form? Where?

OBSERVATIONS AND SUGGESTIONS
   DO NOT DRINK ANY OF YOUR SOLUTIONS.

Writing with iron ink.

Filter a few tablespoons of each of your solutions. In which cases does the precipitate pass through the filter paper? Where can you collect a residue?

If the steel wool looks a little rusty when it is sitting in the tea, add some vinegar and see if you get iron tannate to form. The formation of rust means that the iron has combined with oxygen instead of with tannic acid. Vinegar prevents the iron from combining with oxygen and frees it to combine with tannic acid.

Tannic acid is used to make leather. Soak some leather in water. See if you get a precipitate when you add ferrous sulfate.

In this reaction here's what's happening:

Tannic acid + iron sulfate react to yield iron tannate + sulfuric acid

If you've heard that sulfuric acid is dangerous, you're right. Even though so little forms in this reaction that it can't harm you, do not drink any of these mixtures.

If you write with the iron tannate solution, see if the color of the ink darkens as it is exposed to air. Once this ink was called *blue-black* ink because it is bluish when you write with it but becomes black on exposure to oxygen in the air. Eventually this ink becomes a light brown. The tannate is replaced by oxygen, and the ink is now iron oxide, or rust. Save some "iron ink" for the next experiment.

There Is a Color Change

A fourth way chemists know when a chemical reaction is taking place is that there is a color change. Iron changes from black to reddish brown when it reacts with oxygen to form rust. Silver turns dark gray with tarnish when it comes in contact with sulfurous gases in the air. Copper and brass turn a greenish color in reaction with oxygen and water in the air.

Do the following chemical reactions with inks, visible and invisible, to see some color changes of chemical reactions.

MATERIALS AND EQUIPMENT

paper

crow quill nib and holder or toothpick for writing

"iron ink" from the last experiment

hair dryer (optional)

〰 ☲ ammonia (CAUTION!)

lemon juice

milk

baking soda solution (1 teaspoon in ¼ cup water)

◊ candle or steam iron

PROCEDURE

On paper, write or draw a picture with your iron ink. Let the ink dry. You can use a hair dryer to help it dry faster. Hold the dried writing over some ammonia fumes, which escape from an open ammonia bottle. The ink changes from a blue-black to a brown. Remove the paper from the ammonia. Does the color change again?

Write with "invisible inks" such as lemon juice, milk, or baking soda solution. Let the "ink" dry. CHECK WITH AN ADULT BEFORE DOING THE NEXT STEP. Hold the paper about two inches over the candle flame and pass it back and forth. Be careful just to heat the paper, not to let the flame ignite it. Or you can use a hot iron (set at "cotton") and iron it. What color does your now-visible ink turn?

OBSERVATIONS AND SUGGESTIONS

Here's what's happening to the iron ink. In the presence of ammonia fumes, the iron reacts with oxygen in the air to form iron oxide or rust. When the ammonia is removed, the iron reacts with the tannic acid to form iron tannate again. This is called a *reversible reaction*. There are many reversible reactions in nature.

In the cases of the "invisible inks," the reaction is the same for all. Heat causes other materials in the "inks" to react with the paper and the oxygen in the air, leaving behind the carbon, which shows up as a dark brown or black.

Notice that the products of a chemical reaction are often very different from the reagents that made them.

4. Common Matter

Back in the Middles Ages, in dark and smoky rooms, a few men began to systematically investigate matter. They cooked and distilled and reacted various substances, and developed many techniques used by today's chemists. These early experimenters, known as *alchemists*, did not practice their craft for the joy of knowledge. Instead, they were involved in a "get rich quick" scheme, trying to turn baser metals, such as iron or copper, into gold.

Gold is an unusual substance because it can be found in its pure form in nature. Most other metals are found as ores. An ore is a metal that has combined chemically with another substance and has to be processed to extract the metal. But gold does not react with very many other substances and is called, along with silver and platinum, a *noble* metal because it does not mix and remains pure.

In their attempt to make gold, alchemists sometimes tried mixing gold with unusual and strong reagents. In other experiments they started with copper or iron or some other metal, hoping to turn it into gold. But no matter what they did, gold ended up as gold, and copper or iron never became gold.

It soon became clear to the alchemists that certain substances could not be broken down into simpler substances. These are called *elements*. Elements are the building blocks of all matter. When elements react with each other, they form other substances that no longer have the properties of the elements that made them. These combinations of elements are called *compounds*.

Up to this point, you have been introduced to a few elements and compounds. In this chapter, you'll take a closer look at some of the more common and important elements and compounds in your life.

Splitting Water

Water is such a stable material that early chemists believed it was an element. They did not think water could be broken down into simpler substances. It wasn't until the eighteenth century, when the combustion of certain gases was studied, that water was recognized as a compound of hydrogen and oxygen. It was identified as the product of combustion between "inflammable air" and the "air of kings." "Inflammable air" was later named *hydrogen*, which means "maker of water." *Oxygen* means "acid maker," and breathing it gave one such a good feeling that it was called the *air of kings*.

You know that water is a product of combustion and that combustion is always accompanied by a tremendous release of energy. If you want to reverse the reaction and split water into its elements, you must put energy *into* the water. Heat energy is not practical. Water breaks up only when steam is superheated, something your home lab is not set up to do. But if you add a small amount of electrical energy, you can easily break up a small amount of water, enough to examine the elements that make it up. This is what you'll be doing in the next experiment.

MATERIALS AND EQUIPMENT

    a carbon rod from inside a flashlight battery
    serrated knife or file
    bell wire (from a hardware store)
    scissors
    electrical or masking tape
    measuring spoons
    washing soda (sodium carbonate)
    measuring cup

small, deep bowl
2 paper clips
2 identical small olive jars or test tubes
a 6-volt dry cell battery
wooden toothpicks
◊ kitchen matches
spring clothespin or tongs
plastic coffee can lid

PROCEDURE

Cut the carbon rod in half by carefully scoring it with the knife or file (running the knife or file over the same spot several times to make a groove) and then breaking it in two where you scored it. Cut two lengths of bell wire about 12 inches long. Strip about 1½ inches of the insulation (coating) off each end of the wires. To do this, cut through the insulation with the scissors, being careful not to cut the wire, and pull off the insulation. Wrap one end of each wire around the end of a carbon rod. Cover the connections with tape so no bare wire is exposed. Dissolve a tablespoon of washing soda in about two cups of water. (You'll discover the role of the washing soda in chapter 5.) Your measurements don't need to be exact. You want to make enough solution to fill the bowl and the two olive jars.

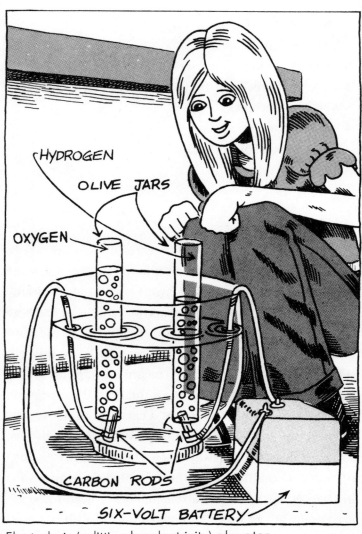

HYDROGEN

OLIVE JARS

OXYGEN

CARBON RODS

SIX-VOLT BATTERY

Electrolysis (splitting by electricity) of water.

Set up your apparatus as shown in the drawing. When you set up, fill each olive jar with washing soda solution and invert it in the bowl so no air is in the jars and each is completely filled. The last thing to do to start your experiment is to complete the circuit by attaching the wires to the battery electrode. The product gases will collect by the displacement of water.

OBSERVATIONS AND SUGGESTIONS

Notice as the gases start to collect in the jars that one jar collects twice as much gas in the same period of time as the other. This ratio of 2:1 is a clue to the makeup of water. There is twice as much hydrogen as oxygen in water. (The reason that hydrogen collects at one carbon rod and oxygen collects at the other will be discussed in the next chapter.) This is evidence of an important law in chemistry called the *Law of Definite Proportions*. It states: When elements combine to form compounds, they do so in fixed proportions indicating a fixed composition.

The composition of a molecule is easiest to see when both the elements making up that molecule are gases. Since there is twice as much hydrogen as oxygen, there must be two atoms of hydrogen for every atom of oxygen in a molecule. The formula for a molecule of water is H_2O. H is the symbol for hydrogen, 2 is a subscript telling how many hydrogen atoms are present, and O is

65

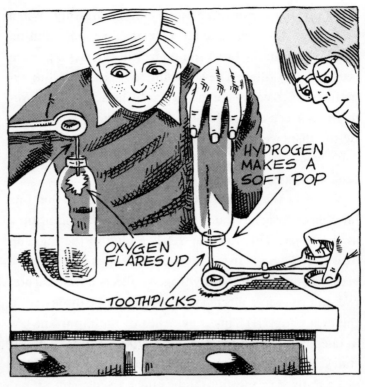

The elements in water have different chemical properties.

the symbol for oxygen. Since there is no subscript for oxygen, the presence of one atom is assumed. More on symbols and formula writing will be given in chapter 6.

When the hydrogen-collecting bottle is filled, test it for hydrogen. Be patient. Collecting enough hydrogen takes time — maybe all day. HAVE AN ADULT WITH YOU

FOR THIS TEST. HYDROGEN IS HIGHLY COM-
BUSTIBLE. Carefully holding the bottle upside down
with tongs, remove it from the water. Since hydrogen is
lighter than air, you can keep it from spilling out by holding the jar upside down. If any oxygen gets mixed in with
the hydrogen, the jar may break. Bring a burning toothpick, held with a spring clothespin or tongs, to the mouth
of the upside-down jar. A soft "pop" is a positive test
for hydrogen. A loud pop means that some air got mixed
in with your hydrogen.

Test the contents of the other jar as you did your test
for oxygen in chapter 3, by inserting a glowing toothpick
held with tongs into the jar. Since oxygen is heavier than
air, keep the jar upside down and slip a plastic lid over
the mouth of it before you remove it from the water.
Holding the lid in place, remove the jar from the water
and turn it right side up when you get it outside. It doesn't
matter if there is still water in the jar.

"Burning" Steel

Many substances combine with oxygen without giving
off enough heat to cause a fire. Iron is one such element.
Do the following experiment to see the formation of iron
oxide, also known as rust, and to see the proportion of
oxygen in the air.

MATERIALS AND EQUIPMENT

◊ candle

◊ kitchen matches

metal pie plate

water

small jar (such as a jelly jar)

steel wool without soap (from a hardware store)

masking tape

vinegar

PROCEDURE

First, repeat the procedure on page 44 and see what happens when the oxygen in the air is used up and water replaces its volume. Drip wax in the middle of the pie plate and set the candle in it so it remains upright. Put water in the pie plate so it is ⅔ full. Light the candle. Cover the burning candle with the jar. Watch what happens shortly after the candle goes out.

Take apart the setup and remove the candle from the pie pan. Stuff some steel wool into the bottom of the jar. You should put in enough so that the steel wool doesn't fall out when you turn the jar upside down. Now remove the steel wool and dip it in vinegar and insert it back into the bottom of the jar. Make sure it stays put. Use masking tape if necessary. Put water in the pie pan as in the last setup and place the jar with the steel wool upside down in the pan. Let this sit for several days as you observe what happens.

OBSERVATIONS AND SUGGESTIONS

The candle goes out when the oxygen in the jar is used up. A small amount of carbon dioxide—one product of combustion—remains in the jar. This small amount of carbon dioxide, however, takes up a lot less room than the amount of oxygen in the air, which is about 20 percent. The water rises in the jar, taking up the space left by the reacting gas.

The rusting of steel wool removes oxygen from the air.

CLAY STOPPER

1/4 FULL OF 3% HYDROGEN PEROXIDE + 1/4 TSP. MANGANESE DIOXIDE

OLIVE JAR

TUBING

Collecting oxygen gas.

70

In the second experiment, iron combines with oxygen to form iron oxide, or rust. No carbon dioxide forms, so the rise of water accurately measures the disappearing oxygen. How would you describe the properties of rust compared with the properties of iron? The most important properties of iron oxide include color and whether or not the substance is attracted by a magnet. In this experiment the vinegar acts as a catalyst. If you wish to compare reaction rates, use two steel wool setups, one with steel wool dipped in vinegar and the other with untreated, dry steel wool.

If you wish to see iron actually burn, try this: Collect a larger quantity of oxygen than you collected when you split water. Make a generating chamber, where the reaction takes place, in a small jar. Punch a hole in the lid for tubing and make the connection airtight with a plastic clay seal. Set up the apparatus as shown in the drawing, collecting a jar of oxygen by the displacement of water. Cover the jar of collected gas with a plastic lid before removing it from the basin of water. Turn the jar right side up. NOW CHECK WITH AN ADULT. Using metal tongs, hold a small piece of steel wool about the size of a dime in a flame until it's glowing. Plunge the glowing steel into the jar of oxygen. Rapid oxidation of the steel gives off a very bright, hot light. Don't touch the glowing steel to the side of the jar as it may crack.

Carbon

Lampblack, or soot that forms when some heat is removed from a flame of burning fuel, is pure carbon. Charred burnt sugar is also carbon, as is the blackened surface of a log that has been burning in a fireplace.

The element carbon is found in nature in several forms. One form is graphite, which you know of as pencil "lead." Another form is diamond. It is interesting that carbon in graphite form is one of the softest of minerals, while diamond is the hardest. Both graphite and diamond are crystalline forms of carbon, and the difference in crystal structure accounts for the tremendous physical differences in color and hardness.

A simple test for carbon is to heat a small sample of a substance in a metal spoon, to see if you can produce charred remains. Be sure to hold the spoon with tongs or a pot holder, as it will get hot. (You may not be able to clean the spoon easily, so be prepared to sacrifice it to your interest in chemistry.) Here is a list of things to check out: sugar, salt, flour, butter, apple, milk.

Nitrogen

Nitrogen was once known as the "lazy" gas because it is slow to enter into chemical reactions. An easy way to produce a relatively pure sample of nitrogen is to go back to the candle-in-the-pie-pan experiment on page 44. First, mix a small amount of washing soda in the water. Then run the experiment. The gas that remains in the jar after the candle goes out and the water has risen is mostly nitrogen with a little carbon dioxide. Now carefully remove the jar without letting in any air. Slip a cover underwater. As you slide it across the mouth of the jar, loosen the candle so that it ends up in the jar. (If you try to remove the candle, you may let in some air.) Screw on the lid while the mouth of the jar is still upside down, underwater. Remove the jar with the lid firmly in place. You will also have some water in the jar, which you want. Shake the jar. The carbon dioxide that is still in the jar will dissolve in the washing soda solution. Nitrogen makes up about 78 percent of the air. Almost 100 percent of the air in the jar will be nitrogen.

But the "laziness" of nitrogen doesn't mean that there aren't plenty of nitrogen compounds around. Household ammonia is a compound of nitrogen and hydrogen. The "laughing gas" dentists use is a compound of nitrogen and oxygen. Proteins — the most complex of molecules and essential to life — are compounds of carbon, hydrogen, oxygen and nitrogen. TNT and fertilizer are also nitrogen compounds.

Unfortunately, a chemical test for nitrogen involves

some extremely hazardous chemicals and procedures, so we can't include them in this book. Later on, we'll do an experiment with ammonia.

Chlorine

Chlorine is a greenish-yellow, heavy *poisonous* gas, with a distinctive, irritating smell. It is highly reactive and is almost never found as an element in nature. There are two important chlorine compounds in most households: sodium chloride, or common table salt, and laundry bleach.

Do the next experiment very carefully to release chlorine gas from household bleach.

MATERIALS AND EQUIPMENT
  measuring spoons
▲ ⚔ liquid laundry chlorine bleach (sodium hypochlorite)
  2 aspirins
  custard cup or small glass dish
  spoon for stirring
  strip of colored cotton cloth

PROCEDURE
  CHECK WITH AN ADULT BEFORE DOING THIS EXPERIMENT. Chlorine gas is irritating and very

poisonous. Even though this experiment does not make enough gas to harm you, don't inhale the chlorine gas.

First, wet the strip of colored cotton cloth with drops of water so that the cloth is not evenly damp. There should be some dry spots.

Put two tablespoons of bleach and the two aspirins in the custard cup. Stir until the aspirins break up. Aspirin manufacturers put an insoluble material in tablets that will settle to the bottom. It has no effect on the experiment. If you look closely you can see tiny bubbles rising

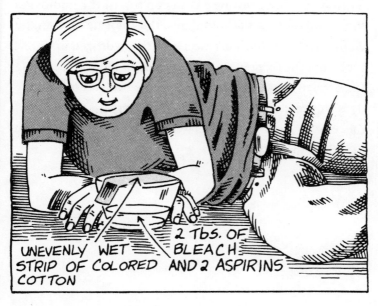

Setup for "Chlorine" experiment.

to the surface of the liquid in the cup. These are bubbles of chlorine. Drape the strip of unevenly moistened cloth over the cup.

OBSERVATIONS AND SUGGESTIONS

Which parts of the cloth are bleached, the wet or the dry areas? Dip the end of the cloth in the mixture. Does it lose its color quickly?

Here's what's going on: The bleach reacts with the acid in aspirin to liberate chlorine gas. Since chlorine is heavier than air, the chlorine gas sits on top of the liquid. As more and more gas accumulates, the chlorine reaches the cloth. Here the chlorine reacts with the hydrogen in water, replacing the oxygen to form hydrogen chloride, freeing the oxygen. Oxygen and free chlorine both react with the dyes in the cloth and chemically alter them to "bleach" the cloth. And yes, this is the way your clothes are bleached in the wash.

5. Electrical Solutions

Electricity was an entertaining mystery to the ancient Greeks. When they rubbed petrified pine sap — which we call *amber* and they called *elektros* — with fur, the amber acquired a novel power. It could now attract other objects, such as bits of fluff. This power of attraction is similar to that of a magnet, but it doesn't last as long or work on the same kinds of materials. Magnets attract iron objects, while rubbed or "charged" amber attracts non-metals. After a while, the amber loses its charge and has to be rubbed again to regain it.

You, too, have experienced electrically charged material. You've felt electrical charges when pulling apart clothes taken immediately from the dryer, or when brushing your hair on a cold, dry wintry day, or when touching a metal doorknob after walking across a rug. This kind of electricity is called *static electricity* because it doesn't move freely. ("Static" means to stay in place.) It is trapped in the material until the charge becomes strong enough to jump through the air to some other object. When static electricity does move through the air, it gives off heat and light energy, and if it is jumping to or from your hand, you feel a small shock.

There are two kinds of static electricity. One kind is labeled *negative* and the other *positive*, depending on what they attract. After being rubbed, the fur has a positive charge and the amber a negative one. Glass, nylon and wool all tend to develop a positive charge, like fur, especially if they are rubbed with polyethylene plastic, Saran wrap or a hard rubber comb. The plastic, Saran wrap and rubber comb become negatively charged. Charged objects will attract certain uncharged objects. And they will attract each other if they have *opposite* charges. When they have the same charge—when both are positive or both are negative—they repel each other.

Static electricity was carefully studied by scientists in the eighteenth century. One question was, "Is lightning a form of static electricity?" That was answered with a resounding "Yes!" by the great statesman and scientist Benjamin Franklin. He reported the discovery, which was made by flying a kite in a thunderstorm. It was not an ordinary kite. A wire stuck out of one end. The other end of the wire was attached to the kite string, which was made of silk. At the end of the string, there was a metal key. Sure enough, when the key was touched, there was a strong electrical shock. Static electricity from the sky had been attracted to the wire and moved through the silk thread to the key. Franklin was lucky he wasn't electrocuted by his experiments with "electrical fire." Early experiments with electricity killed at least one scientist.

Electricity moving though a material, like the silk kite string, is called *current* electricity, and the material it moves through is an electrical *conductor*. Static electricity is attracted to conductors and will become an electric current if a conductor is around. This is the principle of the lightning rod. Lightning strikes the rod, which is made of a conductor, and the electricity in the lightning is conducted harmlessly to the ground.

The ability to conduct electricity is an important physical property chemists look for when describing matter. Elements that conduct electricity are, for the most part, metals. Elements that do not conduct electricity well — that offer *resistance* to an electrical current — are, for the most part, nonmetals. They are often called electrical *insulators*. There are a few elements — for instance, silicon — that conduct electricity under certain conditions; these are called *semiconductors*. Silicon's semiconductor properties allow it to regulate an electric current, making the high technology of computers possible.

Understanding electricity has made an obvious contribution to technology. It's easy to see how electricity makes the light bulb, the telephone, television and countless other devices possible—inventions that have dramatically changed everyday life over the past hundred years. But understanding electricity has done more than the obvious. It has given us insights into the structure of atoms, of the particles that make up atoms and of the nature of chemical bonding to form molecules. Understanding electricity is at the very center of understanding chemistry. In this chapter, you'll experiment with solutions that conduct electricity, to learn how they react with each other; you can apply these principles to plate metal or clean silver.

Electrolyte Current Detector

A battery is a source of electric current. In order for this current to flow, the negatively charged part of the battery—an electrode called the *cathode*—must be connected by a conductor, such as a wire, to the positively charged electrode, the *anode*. This circle of connection, or *circuit*, may include an electrical device such as a light bulb, in order for the battery to be put to work for some useful purpose.

Some water solutions conduct electricity. The solutes

of these solutions are called *electrolytes*. This means that if you put two electrodes in an electrolyte solution and the electrodes are not in contact with each other, the current passes through the solution, completing the circuit. The current conducted by an electrolyte is often very weak. But it can be detected if you put a *galvanometer* into the circuit. A galvanometer is a device that detects a weak electric current. It is worth making, for you will find it has many applications in experiments with electricity. It's also useful for checking out batteries to see if they are still alive.

MATERIALS AND EQUIPMENT
  cardboard
  inexpensive compass (from an army-navy store)
  15 feet of bell wire (from a hardware store)
  string (optional)
  scissors
  6-volt battery

How to Make a Galvanometer

Cut the cardboard into a rectangle that will form a cradle for the compass. Make the cardboard large enough so you can bend the ends up as shown in the picture. Set the compass in the cradle so that the north-south poles on the dial face the folded ends of the cradle. Hold the

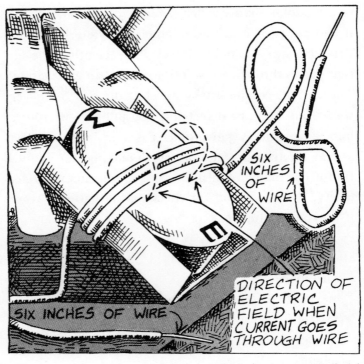

Arrows indicate the direction of the electronic field around the coil. A strong field moves the needle.

compass in place by winding bell wire around the cardboard to form a coil of wire. It will take about 25 turns. Make your coil as compact as possible along the north-south axis. You may wish to tie the wires together with string to hold them in place. (Don't use twist ties, or any other conducting material, however.) Flatten the bottom of your coil so that the compass will rest horizontally and the needle can rotate freely. Leave about six inches of wire free at each end.

Strip the insulation off each wire lead. To do this, gently cut around the plastic insulation with scissors, about ½ inch from the end, being careful not to cut through the wire. When the cut is complete, the insulation will pull off easily.

Test your galvanometer. Set it on the table so that it is perfectly horizontal. Turn it so that the needle is aligned with the north-south axis, parallel to the coil. Touch one bare wire lead to one electrode of the battery. Touch the other lead to the other electrode. The instant swing of the needle indicates current is passing through the coil.

How the Galvanometer Works

A magnet is a piece of iron (usually) that has the ability to attract other, nonmagnetic pieces of iron. If you hang a bar magnet so that it is free to rotate, it will turn so that one end points toward the North Pole of the Earth and the other end points toward the South Pole. This happens because the Earth itself is a magnet with two poles. When two magnets interact with each other, opposite poles attract each other. Thus, the north-seeking pole of a bar magnet will point toward the North Pole of the Earth. The needle of a compass is simply a bar magnet that is free to turn and align with the North Pole. When you turn the dial under it so that the needle hovers over the north-south axis, bingo! You've found your direction.

The area surrounding a magnet through which it exerts its power is called a *magnetic field*. Magnetic fields of different magnets may vary in strength. Obviously, the Earth's magnetic field is a lot more powerful than that of a compass needle. There is a similar field that exists around a wire when a current is passing through it. This is called an *electric field*, and it is quite weak if it comes from a 6-volt battery. You can increase the strength of an electric field by making a coil of wire, as you did on your galvanometer. Every turn of the wire multiplies the strength of the electric field. Of course, the electric field disappears the instant you break the circuit.

When you use your galvanometer, you first line up the needle with the Earth's magnetic field. When a current passes through the wire, it sets up an electric field perpendicular to the magnetic field. If the electric field is *stronger* than the Earth's magnetic field, the needle is displaced. In this way your galvanometer detects currents, including those conducted by electrolytes. Because of the wire coil, which multiplies the strength of the electric field, your galvanometer can detect even extremely weak currents. And, of course, when you increase the number of turns in your coil, you increase the sensitivity of your instrument.

Here's how to use it to detect the ability of a solution to conduct an electric current.

MATERIALS AND EQUIPMENT
   safety pin
   Styrofoam square (cut one from the bottom of a cup)
   mechanical pencil "leads" (graphite sticks)
   electrical tape
   scissors
   bell wire
   various test solutions including: vinegar, ammonia ∯☡,
      baking soda, salt, sugar, orange juice, liquid soap
      and milk of magnesia
   custard cup
   distilled water (optional)

PROCEDURE

With the safety pin, make two holes in a 1½-inch square of Styrofoam about ¼-inch apart. Insert a 2½-inch piece of pencil lead (graphite) in each hole, leaving about ½-inch sticking out of one side. With electrical tape, attach one of the wire leads from your galvanometer to one of the short sides of pencil lead. Make sure the wire and the graphite are in close contact. Cut two 8-inch lengths of bell wire and strip ½-inch off all the ends. Attach one lead to an electrode of the 6-volt

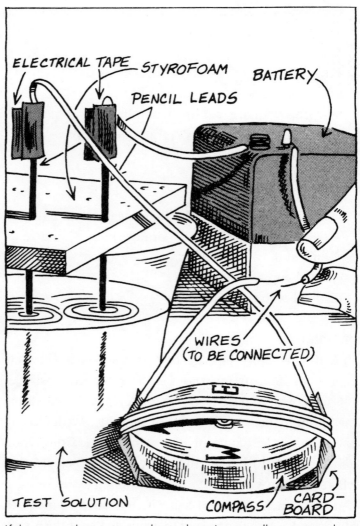

If the test solution is an electrolyte the needle moves when the wires touch.

battery and the other end of that wire to the other pencil lead. Attach one end of the other wire to the other electrode of the battery. The setup should look like the picture.

Put some vinegar, your first test solution, in the custard cup. Insert both pencil leads in the vinegar as shown. Touch the free wire of the galvanometer to the free wire coming from the battery to complete your circuit. Watch the galvanometer needle. If it moves, you know that the circuit is being completed by the vinegar conducting current between the pencil leads.

Empty the vinegar and rinse out the cup well with tap water. Rinse the graphite electrodes, too. Give a final rinse with distilled water, if you have it, to make sure no electrolyte remains in the cup or on the electrodes. (Distilled water is pure and contains no minerals to confuse your results.) Put distilled water in the cup and test to see if it carries a current. The needles should not move. Test each of your other solutions, such as salt water and sugar water, making certain to rinse the cup and your graphite electrodes between tests.

OBSERVATIONS AND SUGGESTIONS

Make a list of all your test solutions and the results of your experiments. Do you get any indications that some solutions are stronger electrolytes than others? Which ones are they?

Acids and Bases

There are two kinds of highly reactive electrolytes that are of great interest to chemists. They were among the substances you tested with your galvanometer. *Acids* have a sour taste and react with some metals to give off hydrogen gas. *Bases* (also called *alkalies*) taste bitter and feel slippery. Since there are a number of acids and bases that are dangerous to handle (they destroy human flesh and are poisonous), chemists don't feel or taste them to determine their nature. Instead, they use a dye called an *indicator*. The color of an indicator depends on whether it is in contact with an acid or a base. One indicator you have already had some experience with is the red cabbage juice you made for your mysterious concoction in chapter 1. It turns pink in acids and green in bases.

In this next experiment you can test various substances around your house with two other indicators. Phenolphthalein (fee-nol-tha-leen) is colorless in acid solutions and bright pink in bases. Turmeric is a spice that stays yellow in acid and turns purplish-brown in base. Make up some more red cabbage juice if you want to have a more complete experiment.

MATERIALS AND EQUIPMENT

hammer

✗ Ex-Lax tablets (your source of phenolphthalein) in cellophane wrappers measuring spoons

☧ rubbing alcohol

paper cups

turmeric or curry powder

"essence of cabbage" (see chapter 1)

plastic straws

white paper napkins or paper toweling

solutions to be tested: vinegar, cream of tartar, baking soda, washing soda, ammonia ☧ ⟨⟨⟨, window cleaner, oven cleaner ▲ ☧ , various juices, salt, sugar, milk of magnesia, Epsom salts.

PROCEDURE

With a hammer, smash the Ex-Lax tablets in their wrappers. Empty the powdered tablets into a paper cup and mix with two tablespoons of rubbing alcohol. Phenolphthalein is more soluble in alcohol than in water. Put ¼ teaspoon turmeric or curry powder in another paper cup and mix with 2 tablespoons of the alcohol. Put some cabbage extract in a third cup to complete your array of test solutions (indicators). Collect the solutions to be tested to see if they are acid or base. Be sure to read all labels carefully before performing the experiment.

Chemists conduct tests with lab instruments called *pipettes*. You can make your own pipettes with straws. Collect a small sample of a solution by dipping the end of a straw into the solution and covering the top of the straw with your finger. Empty your sample onto a piece of a white napkin or paper towel. It will make a wet circle. Using a different straw, put a drop of an indicator (such as phenolphthalein) on top of the wet spot made by your test solution sample. Note the color change, if any. Test the different indicators on each sample. *Use a different straw for each solution and for each indicator.* If you want to be systematic, make up a data sheet as shown and keep track of your results.

OBSERVATIONS AND SUGGESTIONS

Notice that some solutions give a stronger and faster reaction than others. Compare the rate of change between

Data sheet

the baking soda solution and ammonia. Ammonia gives a much more powerful alkali response. When you get such a strong alkali response, drop some vinegar on the spot. See if you can get the indicator to show the color of the acids.

Acids (such as vinegar) and bases (such as milk of magnesia) react with each other. You see this happen when you put vinegar on an indicator in an alkali solution. Such a reaction is called *neutralization*. In a neutralization reaction, an acid reacts with a base to produce water and another electrolyte, called a *salt*. There are many different salts, but you are most familiar with sodium chloride, or common table salt. Sodium chloride forms when hydrochloric acid (a very strong acid) reacts

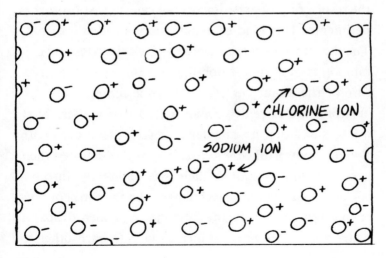

Salt solution

with sodium hydroxide (also known as *lye*, a very strong base). Salt water has no effect on an indicator. It is neutral. On the other hand, the salt of a strong base and a weak acid, like baking soda, will produce a basic reaction, and the salt of a strong acid and a weak base will get an acid response from an indicator. Neutral salts are the same as water — neither acidic nor basic.

Electrolytes and The Structure of Atoms

There comes a time in every science when events that are observed in experiments must be explained by an imaginary picture that describes things that cannot be observed directly. Such an imaginary picture can explain not only the results of past experiments but can suggest future experiments. This kind of explanation is called a *theory*. The theory that explains electricity, electrolytes and certain kinds of chemical bonding is a theory of the structure of the atom. Get ready. Here it comes.

Atoms are extremely small particles of matter. They are so small that no one has ever seen them, even with the most powerful of microscopes. We've detected their presence and measured their size indirectly through sophisticated laboratory techniques. Here's an idea of how small atoms are. Imagine how many ⅛-inch drops of water you would need to line up next to each other to stretch a distance of 62 miles. That's how many atoms are lined up end to end across one of those drops of water!

Interestingly, most of an atom is made up of empty space. At its center, like the sun of our solar system, is the atomic nucleus. It contains most of the mass of the atom and carries a positive electric charge. (The size of an atom's nucleus and its charge varies from element to element, as you will see in chapter 6.) Orbiting the nucleus, like tiny planets, are negatively charged particles called *electrons*. An electron has almost no mass at all, but its negative electrical charge is as strong as the positive charge of the nucleus of the smallest and lightest element—namely, hydrogen.

Electrons are the "currency" of electricity. Atoms lose them or gain them, causing materials to become either positively or negatively charged. In uncharged matter, the number of negative and positive charges are equal. But when amber is rubbed with fur, for example, electrons are rubbed off the fur onto the amber. Amber becomes negatively charged as it accumulates these extra electrons. Meanwhile, the fur that has lost the negatively charged electrons now has a positive charge. The extra positive charges in the atomic nuclei no longer have electrons to balance their numbers. So static electricity is the result of electrons being exchanged between two nonconductors that don't lose or gain electrons easily but, once they do, tend to maintain the imbalance. In current electricity, electrons flow easily and quickly from one atom to another at extremely high speeds. Metals are good electrical conductors precisely because they lose electrons extremely easily.

An electrolyte is a substance that splits or *dissociates* into positively and negatively charged particles when put into water. These charged particles are atoms or groups of atoms that have either lost or gained electrons. They are called *ions*. When a current passes through an electrolyte, the negative ions rush to the positive electrode and the positive ions rush to the negative electrode, completing the circuit of electric current. A nonelectrolyte, such as sugar, does not dissociate into ions in solution and, as a result, will not conduct a current. When you split water in chapter 4, the electric current produced hydrogen ions, which have a positive charge, and oxygen ions, which have a negative charge. The hydrogen went to the negative electrode and the oxygen collected at the positive electrode.

Most acids typically give off hydrogen ions, hydrogen atoms that have lost an electron. Negative ions in bases are strongly attracted to the positive hydrogen ions. These ions are usually one oxygen atom and one hydrogen. When they combine with the hydrogen atom of an acid, water forms. So water is the other product of an acid-base neutralization, along with salt.

Electrical Silver Polish

Tarnish on silver comes from a chemical reaction to sulfur dioxide, a gas that is present in small quantities in the air. The black tarnish of silver sulfide can be removed with the help of an electrolyte and aluminum.

MATERIALS AND EQUIPMENT

stainless steel or enamel (not aluminum) saucepan
aluminum foil
measuring cup
water
measuring spoons
baking soda
salt
tarnished silverware

PROCEDURE

Line the inside of the saucepan with aluminum foil with the shiny side up. Put 4 cups water, 1 tablespoon baking soda, and 1 teaspoon salt into the pan. Put in the tarnished silver. It is important that the silver be placed so as to make as much contact with the aluminum foil as possible and that it is completely covered with the solution. CHECK WITH AN ADULT BEFORE USING THE STOVE. Bring the mixture to a boil. Watch as the tarnish disappears. This may take some time—up to 15 minutes, if any piece is heavily tarnished. Let the silver cool before you remove it from the pan. Rinse it off. Examine the foil in the pan.

OBSERVATIONS AND SUGGESTIONS

Compare the used aluminum foil with unused foil. If the used foil looks tarnished, it's because it now has a coating of aluminum sulfide. Aluminum is more reactive with sulfur than silver is. Your electrolyte, the baking soda, helped the sulfur leave the surface of the silver and react with the aluminum. Here's how:

The hot baking-soda solution breaks up the silver sulfide into ions of silver and ions of sulfur. The silver ions remain on the surface of the silver. But the sulfur ions move through the electrolyte to the surface of the aluminum. Aluminum also loses electrons. These electrons transferred to the silver where the two metals touch, changing the silver ions to silver. The positively charged aluminum ions attract the negative sulfur ions more strongly than the silver ions. So the sulfur combines with the aluminum, forming a dark coating of aluminum sulfide, and the silver becomes clean. The salt makes the solution a stronger electrolyte and helps move the ions.

Electroplating

Metal ions in solution can be deposited as a thin layer of the metal on the surface of another metal — or nonmetal, for that matter. The process by which this is done is called *electroplating*. The deposited material is a layer that closely adheres to the surface. It may be powdery, it may be crystalline, or it may look like another metal. The results depend on a lot of things that can be varied: the voltage, the electrolyte you use, and the material you are plating.

There are lots of ways you can improvise on this electroplating procedure. Have fun! Be careful.

MATERIALS AND EQUIPMENT
  bell wire
  scissors
  a nickel
  6-volt battery
  piece of copper (use a strip of copper or a copper scrubbing pad or a shiny penny)
� ☈ ammonia or copper cleaner
  Windex
  small jar or juice glass

PROCEDURE
Cut two 9-inch lengths of bell wire. Strip about 2 inches off one end and ½ inch off the other of both pieces. Wrap the longer piece of stripped wire around the nickel. Attach the other end of this wire to the negative electrode of a 6-volt battery. The item you are plating—in this case,

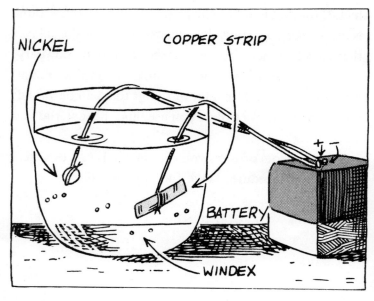

NICKEL

COPPER STRIP

BATTERY

WINDEX

Electroplating

the nickel—now becomes the negative electrode. Wrap the longer stripped end of the second piece of wire around some copper. The copper should be bright and shiny. (Clean it with ammonia or copper cleaner first and rinse well before using.) A strip of copper (from a hardware store) works best, but you can also use any of the other copper items mentioned. Attach the other end of this wire to the positive electrode of the battery. Don't let the nickel and copper touch each other.

Pour enough Windex into the jar so that it is ¾ full.

Hang the nickel and the piece of copper in the solution so that they are about an inch apart but are not touching. Bend the wires over the rim of the glass to hold them in place. Wait. Check the nickel every twenty minutes or so.

OBSERVATIONS AND SUGGESTIONS

Copper, in solution, has a positive charge and will be attracted to the negative electrode. Windex has copper ions in solution. You can tell because of its color; copper ions have a blue-green color. (In this experiment, the copper strip serves only as an electrode, not as a source of copper ions.) As the electroplating takes place, notice that a gas is coming off the nickel. You can collect this gas and test it, but be very careful as you are dealing with a highly poisonous gas. CHECK WITH AN ADULT BEFORE DOING THIS TEST. (Use the method of the displacement of water in an olive jar or test tube. Test for chlorine by gently waving it once toward your nose. A sharp, unpleasant smell like bleach indicates chlorine. The copper salt in solution is probably copper-chlorine compound.) Look at the surface of the positive copper electrode. It will collect a blue-green powdery material. This is also a copper salt. Scrape it off from time to time to keep the electroplating reaction going.

Try copperplating a dime instead of a nickel. Try using a carbon (graphite) electrode instead of a coin. If you can get some copper sulfate (some garden supply stores may have it), use it in solution as your electrolyte. Try other blue cleaning solutions as electrolytes. Try more voltage by using bell wire to connect the negative electrode of another battery to the positive electrode of the battery you are using. Then use another piece of wire to connect the other electrodes.

6. The Language of Chemists

By the time you reach this chapter, you should have some laboratory experience under your belt. So here's where you discover some of the important theories underlying chemistry. There are no experiments in this chapter. But the information and ideas presented here are necessary for you to understand the experiments in the chapters that follow as well as helping you understand more fully the experiments you have already done.

The science of chemistry is like a beautiful tapestry woven from many threads. Each thread represents the work of a particular scientist. Some threads are more noticeable than others; yet most of the threads lose their individuality as they become part of a larger picture. Some scientists have made their contribution by examining the behavior of gases. Others have worked on understanding electricity. Still others labored to list and measure the physical and chemical properties of countless substances. A great many contributions came from the science of physics. And every once in a while, someone came along who pulled together the work of others in a giant breakthrough that gave all the work a larger meaning and pointed new directions for future research.

The big picture of this tapestry of chemistry is one that can't be seen in the real world. It is described in symbols and in the language of mathematics. The basis for all the theories is a model of the atom, thought of as a miniature solar system, of a size so tiny that it is almost impossible to imagine and with behavior that sounds out of this world. It is entirely understandable that you might ask, "How is its behavior known?" If I stopped to answer your question, we would get sidetracked. So much that we know about the atom sounds truly fantastic. Yet I could tell you about laboratory work that was done to discover this information and could be repeated, if you wanted to take the time and trouble and if you had the facilities. Then you would see how one small thread of the big picture is known to be true.

For now, let's take a shortcut while I paint you an outline of the big picture. There are well-established ways of thinking about atoms and how they behave — they are the theories of modern chemistry. These theories are solidly based on detailed laboratory work. It's work you can rely on.

Organizing the Elements

The first step in any science is to identify and describe the basics. In chemistry, this meant zeroing in on the elements. Elements are defined as those substances that cannot be broken down chemically into simpler substances. Elements include nonmetals like carbon, oxygen, hydrogen, nitrogen and chlorine as well as metals like gold, sodium, potassium, iron and copper. By the middle of the nineteenth century, there were more than thirty known elements, enough for chemists to want to move on to the next step in the development of a science — organizing the basics into some kind of meaningful system.

But on what basis? What did gold have in common with carbon or oxygen? One thing all the elements had in common was weight. It was well known that hydrogen was the lightest of the elements. Perhaps the hydrogen atom was the building block of heavier atoms, that atoms of heavier elements were simply multiples of hydrogen atoms. What would happen if you lined up all the elements in order of increasing weight?

This idea occurred to the brilliant Russian chemist Dmitri Mendeleev (men-dal-ay-of), and it resulted in a tremendous breakthrough in the 1870s. Mendeleev discovered that when he arranged the known elements from left to right, in order of increasing weight, every once in a while along came a heavier element with other properties very similar to those of a lighter one. So instead of just listing elements from left to right, Mendeleev put elements with similar properties *under* each other, forming a table. Groups of elements on this table formed families when you looked down a column. For example, the gases fluorine and chlorine, the liquid bromine and the solid iodine all combined with sodium to make similar salts. Mendeleev arranged these elements as one column in his table. Later they were called the *halogen* family meaning "makers of salt." Mendeleev's rule was that when elements are arranged in order of increasing weight, there is a *periodic repetition* of certain properties. The famous *Periodic Table of the Elements* was created.

The Periodic Table you see today is far more complete than it was in Mendeleev's time. All the elements had not yet been discovered. But here's the beauty of his great insight: When Mendeleev laid out his table, he found that he didn't know some of the elements that would fit under others. *So he left gaps.* This told other chemists not only what new elements to look for but also what they would be like. They would have properties similar to those of other members of their families. The science grew explosively as the gaps were filled in. Today's Table is not arranged in order of increasing weight. It is based on a more up-to-date idea of the particles that make up the atom and how they are arranged.

The Structure of the Atom

Chemists think of atoms as being made up of three basic subatomic particles. (Nuclear physicists think in terms of many more.) The center, or *nucleus*, of the atom contains two types of particles and most of the mass of the atom. One particle is the *proton*. A proton has a *positive* electrical charge and is assigned the weight of one atomic mass unit (abbreviated *amu*). This is the weight of the hydrogen atom, the simplest atom of all, with only a proton in its nucleus.

The second nuclear particle has no electric charge—it is electrically neutral—and is called a *neutron*. A neutron has a mass equal to that of a proton, 1 amu.

The third subatomic particle is our old friend the *electron*. An electron has a negative electrical charge equal to the opposite positive charge of a proton. But its mass is so small (1 proton weighs as much as 1,837 electrons) that it has virtually no effect on the total weight of the atom. The number of electrons in an atom is equal to the number of protons. A hydrogen atom has one electron and one proton.

Chemists have defined the number of protons in an

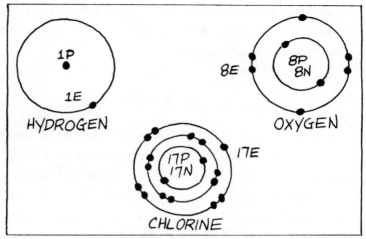

HYDROGEN

OXYGEN

CHLORINE

Hydrogen, chlorine, and oxygen gases are all made of two-atom molecules.

atom as its *atomic number*. Thus the atomic number of hydrogen is 1. *The number of protons in the nucleus — the atomic number — determines what the element is.* If an atom has 8 protons, it is oxygen; if it has an atomic number of 7, it is nitrogen; if it has 47, it is silver. Since the number of protons is equal to the number of electrons, the atomic number tells you the number of electrons in an atom as well as the number of protons.

Since a neutron has the same mass as a proton, it affects an atom's weight. The atomic weight of a single atom is the sum of protons and neutrons in its nucleus. (The mass of the electron is so small that it has no effect on atomic weight, even in elements whose atoms contain many electrons.) An atom of iron has 26 protons and 26 electrons, so its atomic weight is 52. An atom of iodine has 53 of each and an atomic weight of 106. Chlorine has 17 protons, 18 neutrons (and, of course, 17 electrons). The neutron has no effect on what the element is. If you have an atom with 1 proton and 1 neutron, its atomic number is 1 and its atomic weight is 2. It is still hydrogen — actually, "heavy hydrogen." And it behaves chemically exactly like ordinary hydrogen with its single proton nucleus. Varieties of an element that have the same atomic number but different atomic weights due to extra neutrons are called *isotopes*. "Heavy hydrogen" is an isotope of hydrogen. More on isotopes later.

Electrons are like planets, in that they orbit the nucleus. An orbit is a path some distance from the nucleus. As the number of electrons increases, so does the number of orbits. Electron orbits are extremely orderly. Each electron orbit has a maximum number of electrons it can contain. When that number is reached, the next level begins. Here's how it works.

Hydrogen has 1 electron. There is only one electron orbit or shell (also known as an *energy level*). The next element on the Periodic Table, helium, has 2 electrons. Two electrons complete this first energy level, and there can never be more than two in this shell. So the next element, with 3 electrons, has a complete first electron orbit and has 1 electron starting the next energy level. Unlike the first electron shell, the second electron shell can hold more than 2 electrons. It can hold a maximum of 8 electrons. So the succeeding elements, with 4, 5, 6, 7, 8, and 9 electrons, each add an electron to this outer shell until we come to the atom with 10 electrons, neon. Neon has a complete inner shell with 2 electrons and an outer shell with 8 electrons. Eight electrons complete this level. The next element, with 11 electrons, has 2 in its first shell, 8 in its second, and 1 starting its third.

Elements with higher atomic numbers have as many as 7 electron shells, some of them are complete with 18 and 32 electrons.

For the chemist, the electrons that are most important are the ones in the outermost shell, the shell farthest from the nucleus, for these electrons are the ones that are lost, gained or shared in chemical reactions. They are the ones that make possible the bonding between atoms to form molecules.

Chemical Bonds

So far, we've just drawn a picture of the atoms of elements. In their uncombined, or elemental state, the number of electrons equal the number of protons, and there is no overall charge on the atom. But most atoms are not

Diagram of the arrangement of carbon and hydrogen atoms in an octane molecule.

found in nature in their uncombined state. Most atoms are found forming molecules with other atoms. Why is this so?

There is a tendency in all atoms to acquire a stable number of 2 or 8 electrons in their outermost electron shells. This is done by trading or sharing electrons with other atoms. In the process, chemical bonds are made and molecules are formed. Here's a simple example.

The metal sodium (atomic number 11) has 1 electron in its outermost shell. The shell underneath is complete with 8 electrons. Sodium can have a complete outer shell if it *loses* that "odd" eleventh electron. Now take a look at chlorine, with an atomic number of 17. It has 7 electrons in its outer shell. Its outer shell needs only 1 more to be complete. Where could chlorine get such an electron? Enter sodium. A sodium atom gives up 1 electron to a chlorine atom to form the compound sodium chloride, or common table salt. Remember what happens when sodium chloride dissolves in water? The atoms dissociate. Chlorine keeps that electron to become a negative ion, and sodium is stripped of its electron and has a positive charge due to the 1 extra proton in its nucleus. The tendency for these atoms to get a complete outer electron shell is greater than the tendency to remain electrically neutral, with an equal number of protons and electrons.

It is these electrons in the outer shell that are available to be lost or gained during a chemical reaction that determines the chemical behavior of an element. So chemists give them a number called the *valence*. The valence number is the same as the charge on an atom when it has completed its outermost shell. Chlorine has a valence of -1 because it gains 1 electron that gives it a negative charge. Sodium has a valence of +1 because it *loses* 1 electron, keeping the extra charge of 1 proton. Some atoms have a valence of +2, because they lose 2 electrons. Others have a valence of -2, gaining 2 electrons. Still other atoms have variable valences and may lose 2 or 3 or more electrons or gain 2 or 3 or more electrons. Compounds that are formed from such an *exchange* of electrons are examples of *ionic* bonding. All electrolytes have ionic bonds.

A second type of bonding involves a *sharing* of outer electrons, as opposed to an exchange. A simple example of this bond occurs with the element hydrogen. A single hydrogen atom has only 1 electron. If two hydrogen atoms share their 2 electrons equally, the first electron shell is complete for both atoms. So, in nature, hydrogen is a gas made up of hydrogen *molecules* of 2 hydrogen atoms held together by a *covalent* bond.

Atoms with 4 electrons in their outer shells, such as carbon, tend to form covalent bonds. Carbon can form a covalent bond with other carbon atoms, to make chains and rings and endless varieties of patterns, sometimes becoming giant molecules. There is a branch of chemistry, called *organic chemistry,* based entirely on carbon compounds.

Some elements, under certain circumstances, can form covalent bonds as well as ionic. Two oxygen atoms with 6 outer electrons are more comfortable sharing 4 electrons of their outer shells with each other than they are existing as single atoms. So in its natural state, the element oxygen is made up of oxygen molecules, consisting of 2 oxygen atoms. Similarly, nitrogen gas and chlorine and fluorine gas also exist as two-atom (*diatomic*) molecules in nature.

There are a number of groups of atoms that are chemically bonded to each other, that act together as if they

111

were a single atom when making compounds. These groups are called *radicals*, and they also have valence numbers. Some of the names of radicals will sound familiar to you:

SULFATE is a group of one sulfur atom and four oxygens; its valence is -2.

PHOSPHATE has one phosphorus and four oxygens; its valence is -3.

CARBONATE has one carbon and three oxygens; its valence is -2.

HYDROXIDE has one oxygen and one hydrogen; its valence is -1.

BICARBONATE has one carbon, one hydrogen and three oxygens; its valence is -1.

AMMONIUM has one nitrogen and four hydrogens; its valence is +1.

Symbols, Formulas, and Equations

Chemists would have a hard time trying to communicate about elements, compounds and chemical reactions by writing everything out in English. So they have developed a shorthand to make things simpler. And it really does, if you give it a chance.

Every element has a symbol in the form of a *capital*

letter and, in some cases, a second, lowercase letter. Usually the capital letter is the initial letter of the name of the element in English or in Latin. You can see all the symbols for all the elements on the Periodic Table of the Elements on page 116. Here are some symbols for some of the more common elements: H, Na, Mg, Fe, Ni, Cu, Al, C, N, Ag, Au, Hg, U, K, Mn, P, S. Do you know what they are? They stand for: hydrogen, sodium, magnesium, iron, nickel, copper, aluminum, carbon, nitrogen, silver, gold, mercury, uranium, potassium, manganese, phosphorus and sulfur.

Chemists use these symbols to write *formulas* for compounds. A formula tells what atoms and *how many* of each are in 1 molecule of a compound. The number that tells how many atoms it contains is written as a subscript just below and to the right of the symbol for that atom. If there is no subscript, only 1 atom of that element is present in that formula. The formula for sodium chloride is NaCl. Here are some others:

H_2O = water
$NaHCO_3$ = sodium bicarbonate (baking soda)
CO_2 = carbon dioxide
H_2SO_4 = sulfuric acid
KOH = potassium hydroxide
H_2O_2 = hydrogen peroxide

Chemical formulas are used to tell what happens in a chemical reaction. Numbers that appear before a formula tell how many molecules are involved in a reaction. For example:

$$2H_2 + O_2 \rightarrow 2H_2O$$

This means that 2 molecules of hydrogen gas and 1 molecule of oxygen gas react to yield 2 molecules of water.

Reading the Periodic Table

The Periodic Table on pages 116 is a useful tool for the working chemist. It gives a great deal of information. Each box is a summary of an element. It includes the symbol of the element, its name, its atomic number, its atomic weight and the number of electrons in each energy level. Notice that the atomic weight is usually not a neat, round number but a fraction. This is because atomic weights are determined by measuring a sample of the element as it exists in nature. The atomic weight on the Periodic Table is an average of a very large number of atoms. For many elements, a pure sample contains isotopes. Some atoms weigh more than others.

You'll recall that an isotope is an atom with the same number of protons as another atom but with a different number of neutrons. In a sample of hydrogen gas, for example, a small percentage of hydrogen atoms has 1 extra neutron and an even smaller fraction has 2, with an atomic weight of 3. When a natural sample of hydrogen gas is weighed and the average weight is found for 1 atom, the heavier hydrogen isotopes make the average slightly more than 1 amu. Some of the isotopes of heavier elements, like uranium, are radioactive. One particular isotope of uranium is used as fuel in nuclear reactors. Its atomic weight is given as a superscript after its symbol. U^{238} and U^{235} are 2 isotopes of uranium. U^{235} is used as fuel for nuclear reactors and in atom bombs.

Rows across the Periodic Table are *periods*. Moving from left to right, each element has 1 more electron than the preceding element. The first period has 2 elements; the second and the third periods have 8 each. The fourth and fifth periods have 18 elements each. The fifth period has 32 elements, and the sixth is incomplete with 19 elements. There are 92 elements occurring in nature and 13 manmade elements.

The vertical columns are called families of elements, the members of which have related properties. On the far right is the family of noble gases. These six elements have complete outer electron shells. As a result, they do not form chemical bonds with other elements and are always found in nature in a pure state. They are also called the *inert gases*.

At the far left is Group I, known as the *alkali metals*.

PERIODIC CHART OF THE ELEMENTS

KEY

	← Atomic Number
79	
Au	← Atomic Symbol
+1 +3	Oxidation States
196.9665	← Atomic Weight
-32-18-1	← Electron Configuration

Transition Elements

Orbital	IA	IIA	IIIB	IVB	VB	VIB	VIIB	VIIIB			IB	IIB	IIIA	IVA	VA	VIA	VIIA	VIIIA
	1 -1 +1 **H** 1.0079 1																	2 **He** 4.00260 2 Noble Gases
2	3 +1 **Li** 6.941 2-1	4 +2 **Be** 9.01218 2-2											5 +2 +1 **B** 10.81 2-3	6 +2 +4 **C** 12.011 2-4	7 -3,-2,-1,+1,+2,+3,+4,+5 **N** 14.0067 2-5	8 -2 **O** 15.9994 2-6	9 -1 **F** 18.998403 2-7	10 **Ne** 20.179 2-8
2-8	11 +1 **Na** 22.98977 2-8-1	12 +2 **Mg** 24.305 2-8-2											13 +3 **Al** 26.98154 2-8-3	14 +2 +4 **Si** 28.0855 2-8-4	15 -3 +3 +5 **P** 30.97376 2-8-5	16 -2 +4 +6 **S** 32.06 2-8-6	17 -1 +1 +5 +7 **Cl** 35.453 2-8-7	18 **Ar** 39.948 2-8-8
2-8-8	19 +1 **K** 39.0983 -8-8-1	20 +2 **Ca** 40.08 -8-8-2	21 +3 **Sc** 44.9559 -8-9-2	22 +2 +3 +4 **Ti** 47.88 -8-10-2	23 +2 +3 +4 +5 **V** 50.9415 -8-11-2	24 +2 +3 +6 **Cr** 51.996 -8-13-1	25 +2 +3 +4 +6 +7 **Mn** 54.9380 -8-13-2	26 +2 +3 **Fe** 55.847 -8-14-2	27 +2 +3 **Co** 58.9332 -8-15-2	28 +2 +3 **Ni** 58.69 -8-16-2	29 +1 +2 **Cu** 63.546 -8-18-1	30 +2 **Zn** 65.38 -8-18-2	31 +3 **Ga** 69.72 -8-18-3	32 +2 +4 **Ge** 72.59 -8-18-4	33 -3 +3 +5 **As** 74.9216 -8-18-5	34 -2 +4 +6 **Se** 78.96 -8-18-6	35 -1 +5 **Br** 79.904 -8-18-7	36 **Kr** 83.80 -8-18-8
2-8-18	37 +1 **Rb** 85.4678 -18-8-1	38 +2 **Sr** 87.62 -18-8-2	39 +3 **Y** 88.9059 -18-9-2	40 +4 **Zr** 91.22 -18-10-2	41 +3 +5 **Nb** 92.9064 -18-12-1	42 +6 **Mo** 95.94 -18-13-1	43 +4 +6 +7 **Tc** (98) -18-13-2	44 +3 **Ru** 101.07 -18-15-1	45 +3 **Rh** 102.9055 -18-16-1	46 +2 +4 **Pd** 106.42 -18-18-0	47 +1 **Ag** 107.868 -18-18-1	48 +2 **Cd** 112.41 -18-18-2	49 +3 **In** 114.82 -18-18-3	50 +2 +4 **Sn** 118.69 -18-18-4	51 -3 +3 +5 **Sb** 121.75 -18-18-5	52 +4 +6 +2 **Te** 127.60 -18-18-6	53 -1 +1 +5 +7 **I** 126.9045 -18-18-7	54 **Xe** 131.29 -18-18-8
2-8-18-18	55 +1 **Cs** 132.9054 -18-8-1	56 +2 **Ba** 137.33 -18-8-2	57-71 See Lanthanides	72 +4 **Hf** 178.49 -32-10-2	73 +5 **Ta** 180.9479 -32-11-2	74 +6 **W** 183.85 -32-12-2	75 +4 +6 +7 **Re** 186.207 -32-13-2	76 +3 +4 **Os** 190.2 -32-14-2	77 +3 +4 **Ir** 192.22 -32-15-2	78 +2 +4 **Pt** 195.08 -32-16-2	79 +1 +3 **Au** 196.9665 -32-18-1	80 +1 +2 **Hg** 200.59 -32-18-2	81 +1 +3 **Tl** 204.383 -32-18-3	82 +2 +4 **Pb** 207.2 -32-18-4	83 +3 +5 **Bi** 208.9804 -32-18-5	84 +2 +4 **Po** (209) -32-18-6	85 -1 +1 +5 **At** (210) -32-18-7	86 **Rn** (222) -32-18-8
2-8-18-32	87 +1 **Fr** (223) -18-8-1	88 +2 **Ra** 226.0254 -18-8-2	89-103 See Actinides	104 (261) -32-10-2	105 (262) -32-11-2	106 (263) -32-12-2												

Lanthanides	57 +3 **La** 138.9055 -18-9-2	58 +3 +4 **Ce** 140.12 -20-8-2	59 +3 **Pr** 140.9077 -21-8-2	60 +3 **Nd** 144.24 -22-8-2	61 +3 **Pm** (145) -23-8-2	62 +2 +3 **Sm** 150.36 -24-8-2	63 +2 +3 **Eu** 151.96 -25-8-2	64 +3 **Gd** 157.25 -25-9-2	65 +3 **Tb** 158.9254 -27-8-2	66 +3 **Dy** 162.50 -28-8-2	67 +3 **Ho** 164.9304 -29-8-2	68 +3 **Er** 167.26 -30-8-2	69 +3 **Tm** 168.9342 -31-8-2	70 +2 +3 **Yb** 173.04 -32-8-2	71 +3 **Lu** 174.967 -32-9-2

Actinides	89 +3 **Ac** 227.0278 -18-9-2	90 +4 **Th** 232.0381 -18-10-2	91 +5 +4 **Pa** 231.0359 -20-9-2	92 +3 +4 +5 +6 **U** 238.0289 -21-9-2	93 +3 +4 +5 +6 **Np** 237.0482 -22-9-2	94 +3 +4 +5 +6 **Pu** (244) -24-8-2	95 +3 +4 +5 +6 **Am** (243) -25-8-2	96 +3 **Cm** (247) -25-9-2	97 +3 +4 **Bk** (247) -27-8-2	98 +3 **Cf** (251) -28-8-2	99 +3 **Es** (252) -29-8-2	100 +3 **Fm** (257) -30-8-2	101 +2 +3 **Md** (258) -31-8-2	102 +2 +3 **No** (259) -32-8-2	103 **Lr** (260) -32-9-2

Note: Atomic weights are those of the most commonly available long-lived isotopes based on the 1979 IUPAC Atomic Weights of the Elements. A value given in parentheses denotes the mass number of the

SYMBOLS OF THE ELEMENTS

Ac=Actinium	Co=Cobalt	In=Indium	Os=Osmium	Sm=Samarium
Ag=Silver	Cr=Chromium	Ir=Iridium	P=Phosphorus	Sn=Tin
Al=Aluminum	Cs=Cesium	K=Potassium	Pa=Protactinium	Sr=Strontium
Am=Americium	Cu=Copper	Kr=Krypton	Pb=Lead	Ta=Tantalum
Ar=Argon	Dy=Dysprosium	La=Lanthanum	Pd=Palladium	Tb=Terbium
As=Arsenic	Er=Erbium	Li=Lithium	Pm=Promethium	Tc=Technetium
At=Astatine	Es=Einsteinium	Lu=Lutetium	Po=Polonium	Te=Tellurium
Au=Gold	Eu=Europium	Lr=Lawrencium	Pr=Praseodymium	Th=Thorium
B=Boron	F=Fluorine	Md=Mendelevium	Pt=Platinum	Ti=Titanium
Ba=Barium	Fe=Iron	Mg=Magnesium	Pu=Plutonium	Tl=Thallium
Be=Beryllium	Fm=Fermium	Mn=Manganese	Ra=Radium	Tm=Thulium
Bi=Bismuth	Fr=Francium	Mo=Molybdenum	Rb=Rubidium	U=Uranium
Bk=Berkelium	Ga=Gallium	N=Nitrogen	Re=Rhenium	Unp=Unnilpentium
Br=Bromine	Gd=Gadolinium	Na=Sodium	Rh=Rhodium	Unq=Unnilquadium
C=Carbon	Ge=Germanium	Nb=Niobium	Rn=Radon	V=Vanadium
Ca=Calcium	H=Hydrogen	Nd=Neodymium	Ru=Ruthenium	W=Tungsten
Cd=Cadmium	He=Helium	Ne=Neon	S=Sulfur	Xe=Xenon
Ce=Cerium	Hf=Hafnium	Ni=Nickel	Sb=Antimony	Y=Yttrium
Cf=Californium	Hg=Mercury	No=Nobelium	Sc=Scandium	Yb=Ytterbium
Cl=Chlorine	Ho=Holmium	Np=Neptunium	Se=Selenium	Zn=Zinc
Cm=Curium	I=Iodine	O=Oxygen	Si=Silicon	Zr=Zirconium

These metals are all shiny and are good conductors of heat and electricity. They are also highly reactive. They are called alkali metals because they all react with water to form alkalies and release hydrogen gas.

The elements in Group II are called the *alkaline-earth metals*. As metals they are not as soft as those in Group I. They easily lose the 2 electrons in their outer shells, often to oxygen. There are lots of oxides formed from this group.

Between Groups II and III are the *transition elements*. They have large atomic numbers and at least four energy levels. Something interesting happens as you move across the Table in the transition elements. The outer shell is started with 1 or 2 electrons. Then electrons are added to the shell just under the outer shell. Since the transition elements all have 1 or 2 valence electrons, their chemical behavior is all very similar. The transition elements are all metals, some of which we can see on bumpers of cars, in coins and in jewelry.

Group III is made up of elements with 3 electrons in the outer shell. The top element, boron, is called a semimetal. It has some metallic properties, especially at high temperatures, but it also forms covalent bonds, a property of nonmetals. All the other elements in Group III are metals.

The elements in Group IV have the largest variety of properties of any family. They all have 4 electrons in their outer shells. Should they lose or gain? Mostly they share. Carbon — a nonmetal, as I've mentioned — is the basis of organic chemistry. Silicon is never found in a free state in nature. It is the second most abundant element in the Earth's crust after oxygen, with which it is often combined. Silicon dioxide is the mineral quartz, and is familiar to you as sand and glass.

Group VI has 2 especially important elements, oxygen and sulfur. Both combine with themselves in several forms. Oxygen gas is O_2. But there is also an O_3, known as *ozone*. Ozone has a sharp odor; you may have smelled it near an electrical short circuit. Ozone is located mostly in the upper atmosphere, where it filters out the harmful ultraviolet light from the sun. Sulfur was called *brimstone* in the old days meaning "burning stone" because it burned and produced a choking, smelly gas that made people think of hell. Sulfur is used to make rubber hard. It is used in matches, gunpowder and, most importantly, sulfuric acid, a corrosive chemical used for many industrial processes.

The halogens make up Group VII. The name means "salt former" as mentioned earlier. They all have 7 electrons in their outer shells and form ionic bonds with metals to produce salts. They combine with hydrogen to form acids. In their uncombined state all the halogens are poisonous and highly reactive.

The noble gases of Group VIII were difficult to detect

because they don't react with any other element. Helium was discovered on the sun because it absorbed certain wavelengths of light. Neon is used in decorative electric light tubes because it glows red when a current is passed through it. Most of the light bulbs you use in your home are filled with the noble gas argon.

7. The Chemist Detective

Nowadays, when working chemists wonder what a substance is made of, they have lots of tools available to find out. The goal is to determine the chemical formula of a substance. So chemists run tests that tell what elements and what radicals are present in the substance and how much of each is there. (Tests that measure "how much" are quite sophisticated and require sensitive laboratory instruments.)

Some of these tests you already know. You know how to use an indicator to test for the presence of an acid or base. You know how to use a wood splint to test for the presence of various gases. If a glowing splint bursts into flame, you've got oxygen. If it goes out, you're probably dealing with carbon dioxide. If it makes a small pop, your sample is hydrogen.

There are other tests you can perform in your kitchen laboratory. You can be a chemist detective. That's what this chapter is about.

The Flame Test

When certain metals and their compounds are heated in a flame, they give the flame a distinctive color. This color is a way of identifying the metal. This principle is behind the brilliant colors of fireworks.

MATERIALS AND EQUIPMENT

    cotton swabs

〃 ✗ denatured alcohol

  ◊ candle

    cup of water

    as many of the following as you can collect: salt, cream of tartar, washing soda, boric acid ✗ , powdered copper cleaner, pennies

PROCEDURE

Since this test involves fire, CHECK WITH AN ADULT BEFORE YOU BEGIN. Be sure and keep the bottle of alcohol away from the flame.

Dip the end of a cotton swab in alcohol, then dip it in one of your powders. Stick the end in a flame, and remove it, allowing it to burn. Look for colors in the

The color of the flame indicates the metal ion.

flame. It helps to have the lights dimly lit. Douse the flame in the cup of water.

To test for copper, mix a few drops of water into a small amount of powdered copper cleaner to make a paste. Rub the paste on a penny. Test some of the paste by burning it on the end of a cotton swab that you have dipped in alcohol.

OBSERVATIONS AND SUGGESTIONS

The colors given off by metals are as follows:

sodium — bright yellow
calcium — orange
boron — green
copper — bright green

One problem with this test is that if there is any sodium

present, its strong yellow color will mask the colors of other metals. You may be able to improve the visibility of colors if you dip the end of the alcohol-soaked swab in ammonium chloride (known as sal ammoniac to your pharmacist). Ammonium chloride becomes a white smoke when heated, which enhances the visibility of the colors in a flame. You also might try dipping the swab in a little vinegar before dipping it into the alcohol.

Speaking of pharmacists, it helps to have a friendly one. Perhaps you can make friends by sharing your interest in chemistry. If so, you might be able to buy all sorts of hard-to-get chemicals, like sal ammoniac, or get other samples with interesting metals to test. Be sure to let him or her know that you intend to use these compounds only for your chemistry experiments.

Chromatography

The word "chromatography" means "to write with color." Some colored material in solution will move across a surface, such as paper, with different speeds. You see this as different-colored areas on the paper. Since different pigments have different molecular weights and move at different rates, chromatography is useful for separating different-colored compounds and for identifying unknown compounds by comparing the rates at which they move with known compounds.

MATERIALS AND EQUIPMENT

coffee filter paper

scissors

clean mayonnaise jar

Scotch tape

pencil

fresh spinach or beet leaves

2 custard cups

▲ ⚒ nail polish remover

spoon

small square of clean cloth for straining

wooden toothpicks

hair dryer (optional)

▲ ⚒ lacquer thinner

PROCEDURE

Cut a strip of filter paper 1-inch wide and long enough to almost reach the bottom of the jar with the top end folded over so that it can be held in place later by a strip of tape across the mouth of the jar, as shown in the drawing. Draw a straight line with a pencil about 1 inch from the unfolded end.

Next, extract the pigment from the spinach or beet leaves. It is this colored material that you are going to analyze by chromatography. First, mince the leaves by cutting them up with the scissors into a custard cup. Make the pieces as fine as possible. Pour in a small amount of nail polish remover, enough to wet the minced leaves, and mush the mixture with a spoon. Notice that the green pigment will come out in the solvent. Strain the leaves in the cloth, saving the solvent with the extracted pigment. The nail polish remover should be deep green.

Dip the toothpick into the leaf extract and touch the wet end to the line on the filter paper. You want to make a dot of leaf extract about ¼-inch in diameter. Let the dot dry or dry it with a hair dryer. Make repeated applications of the extract at least 5 or 6 times until it is dark green.

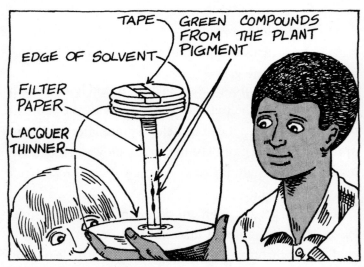

Chromotography experiment.

Put about ½-inch of laquer thinner in the jar. Hang the filter paper in the jar so that the end is submerged in the lacquer thinner but that the spot of plant pigment is above the surface. Do not disturb your experiment for about an hour.

OBSERVATIONS AND SUGGESTIONS

The filter paper acts like a wick, absorbing the lacquer thinner so that it moves up the paper. When the lacquer thinner reaches the plant pigment, it carries the pigment along with it. Since different compounds will be carried along the filter paper at different rates, chromatography can separate these compounds. And, since your are analyzing colored compounds, it's easy to see the separation. As it turns out, green plant pigment is made up of more than one green compound. Since one of these travels faster than the other, you will get at least two clearly defined green spots on your filter paper.

You can use this technique to see if the green pigments in different plants are the same. You can also use it to test red plant pigments, like the one you extracted in the "Essence of Cabbage" experiment. If you do chromatography on red pigments, instead of using nail polish remover and lacquer thinner as your solvent, use water both to extract the pigment and in the jar.

Chromatography may be used to separate any colored

compounds. You just have to make sure that you use the proper solvent. Water or alcohol works well for food coloring and inks. Nail polish remover may have to be used for ballpoint pen ink.

Test for Sugar

A sugar is a compound of carbon, hydrogen and oxygen. It belongs to the group of nutrients called *carbohydrates*. Sugars taste sweet and are a source of energy for your body. Some sugars have the ability to give up 2 electrons. Copper ions eagerly accept 2 electrons, and when they do, they lose their ionized state and become copper metal — a great thing for chemists because there is a dramatic color change. Copper ions are blue, and copper metal is red. So if a color change from blue to red occurs, because the sugar gives up electrons to the copper, a chemist can tell that the sugar is present.

Disappointingly, one sugar that does not reduce copper ions to copper metal is ordinary table sugar, sucrose. But you can use the simple sugars found in fruits and honey for this test.

Here are two ways you can do the test. You can make up your own test solution, or you can use Fantastik cleaning solution. The test solution must contain copper ions in an alkali solution.

▲Fantastik or if you plan to make your own solution, you will need: copper scrubbing pad or copper pennies, a jar with a lid, ammonia ✗ ⌇⌇ , washing soda and measuring spoons

heat-resistant custard cups

pot holders or tongs

food samples such as: honey or syrup, soda cracker, lemon, grapefruit, apple, banana, grapes, jellies, breads, cakes, etc.

PROCEDURE

Before you do this test, CHECK WITH AN ADULT, AS YOU'LL BE USING THE STOVE.

You can use Fantastik as your test solution or make your own solution. The color change is much more dramatic in homemade test solution. To make your own test solution, put the copper scrubbing pad or 4 or 5 pennies in a jar containing about ¼ cup of ammonia. Put the lid on the jar and let it stand overnight or until the solution is dark blue.

When the solution is ready, bring a cup of water to a boil, then remove it from the heat. Add a teaspoon of washing soda to the water. When the washing soda solution is cool, add 2 tablespoons of the ammonia-copper solution to it and mix. This is your alkaline copper-ion testing solution for sugar. Save the ammonia-copper mixture to make more test solution in the future. Keep the jar tightly closed.

If you use Fantastik, pour enough in a custard cup so that you can see its light blue color.

Put about ¼ teaspoon of syrup or honey into the Fantastik or into approximately 2 tablespoons of your homemade test solution. Heat the mixture until it comes to a boil and then let it boil for a few seconds. Then remove from the heat. The Fantastik will turn a reddish yellow and the homemade solution will turn dark red: These are positive tests for sugar. Look for this color change when you test unknowns.

Repeat the procedure with a small sample of another food you want to test in a fresh batch of test solution. Make sure the solution boils briefly. Look for the color change that is a positive test for sugar.

WARNING: DO NOT EAT ANY OF THESE EXPERIMENTS.

OBSERVATIONS AND SUGGESTIONS

There is an enzyme in your saliva that changes starch to sugar. See for yourself. Test a fresh piece of soda cracker for sugar in a test solution. You should have a negative test. Chew another soda cracker. Hold it in your mouth for five minutes, mixing it well with saliva. Test a small sample of the chewed cracker for sugar. You should now get a positive result.

Test for Starch

A starch molecule is a chain of sugar molecules. Unlike sugars, starches are not very soluble in water. But they absorb water and swell, making them useful as gravy thickeners and as pastes.

Starches form a blue-black colored complex with iodine. This is the basis of a chemist's test for starch. Simply put a few drops of iodine from the medicine chest on a food sample. Note: Iodine is POISONOUS so don't put any of these experiments in your mouth. Throw away all food samples when you have finished the experiment. If the red-brown color of the iodine turns blue-black, you know starch is present.

Try testing pure starches, like corn and potato, various baked goods, and other foods such as fruits, vegetables and meats.

Test for Vitamin C

The need for Vitamin C in the diet was discovered hundreds of years ago when people came down with a dread disease known as "spring sickness" or "scurvy." The symptoms included bleeding gums and loose teeth, aching joints and sores on the skin and in the stomach. The disease can be avoided by adding citrus fruits and sauerkraut to the diet. The British navy required that these foods be taken on long ocean voyages, because sailors were particularly susceptible to the disease. For this reason British sailors came to be known as "limeys," after the limes and lemons they were required to eat.

It was not until 1932 that the pure Vitamin C was made in a laboratory. It turned out to be a fairly simple compound. It was named *ascorbic*—meaning "without scurvy"—acid. Ascorbic acid is water-soluble and picks up electrons easily, which makes it easy to detect in a lab test.

MATERIALS AND EQUIPMENT
   measuring cup and spoons
   cornstarch
   knife
   spoons for stirring
   stainless steel or enamel saucepan
   2 jars with lids and labels
▲ ☿ iodine
   250-milligram vitamin C tablet
   small juice glasses or test tubes
   medicine droppers or straws to be used as pipettes

PROCEDURE

This test will not only tell you if vitamin C is present, but if you measure carefully it will also give you an indication of how much of the vitamin is present.

First, make a starch stock solution. To do this, take ½ level teaspoon of cornstarch and pass the back of the knife over the spoon to make the measurement level; then put the cornstarch in the saucepan. Add 1 cup water. CHECK WITH AN ADULT BEFORE USING THE STOVE. Heat and stir until the starch is dissolved. Pour the mixture in one of the jars and let it cool.

Next, make your test solution. Put one teaspoon of the stock starch solution in a clean jar with one cup of water. Add four drops of iodine. The blue color is the result of

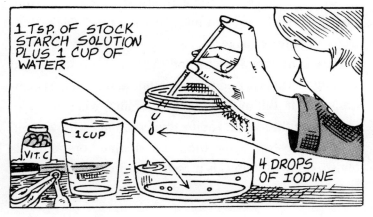

Test for vitamin C.

the starch-iodine complex and is typical of the iodine reaction to starch. It is very diluted in this solution.

To check your test solution, do a positive vitamin C test. Dissolve one 250-milligram vitamin C tablet in one cup of water. Put 2 tablespoons of your test solution in a small glass. Add 1 drop of the vitamin C solution. Stir. If there is no change, add a second drop. The color is gone. See what a sensitive test this is!

OBSERVATIONS AND SUGGESTIONS

Test various foods for vitamin C. Here are some suggestions: fruit and vegetable juices, water extracts of fresh fruits, water extracts of liver (soak a piece of raw liver to make an extract), water extract of pine needles, milk. If you use a pipette to add extracts to stach-iodine solution, practice letting out one drop at a time. See how to use a pipette on page 24.

Here's the chemistry behind the test. Both starch and vitamin C will give electrons to iodine and combine chemically with it. But of the two, the vitamin C will react more easily than the starch. Iodine that combines with vitamin C has no color, while the starch-iodine compound is bluish. So if vitamin C is present, the product that forms is colorless.

Note: Iodine is highly reactive and will accept electrons from many substances. This is the basis of the "ink" to "water" trick in the next chapter on page 144.

Photochemistry

So far, you have seen chemical reactions that involve heat and chemical reactions that involve electricity. You have learned that all chemical reactions involve energy. Some take up energy, and some give off energy. And although heat and electricity seem very different from each other, physicists have shown that all forms of energy are basically the same. Heat, electricity, light and motion are all forms of energy, and one can be transformed into another. (A toaster, for example, transforms electricity into heat.) So far, you have not experienced a chemical reaction that involves light energy. Now you will. The reaction in the next experiment is called a *photochemical* reaction ("photo" means *light*).

The best-known photochemical reactions are in photography and X-rays, and in photosynthesis. Here are some simple activities to introduce you to photochemistry.

How to Make a Photographic Wet Plate

You will need a small silver or silver-plated tray, some silver polish, iodine and an opaque object. (Don't worry, you can polish away the results of your experiment with no harm to the tray.) Polish the silver so it is bright and shining. In dim light, flood the surface of the tray with iodine. Pour off the iodine (still in dim light) and while the tray is still wet, put some object (a key, for instance) on it. Place the tray in bright light for a few minutes. Lift off the object. You should see a silhouette where the object was. The silhouette will quickly fade.

The light causes the iodine and silver to form a dark compound. The area under your object will be lighter because this part of the tray was unexposed to light. Modern film is made of silver salts that also turn dark when exposed to light. Photographers preserve the image in the silver-iodine complex on their film with *hypo*.

Photosynthesis in a Leaf

Cover a part of a leaf of a house plant by placing it between two small cardboard squares and clipping the cardboard together. Put the plant in the sun. Wait two days.

Pinch off your experimental leaf. Remove the green pigment, chlorophyll. HAVE AN ADULT WITH YOU WHEN DOING THE NEXT STEPS. To do this, first put the leaf in boiling water for a few minutes. Then put it in a dish of warm rubbing alcohol. (To prevent the alcohol from catching on fire, heat the alcohol by putting the dish containing alcohol in a pot of warm water. You then heat — but do not boil — the pot of water.) The chlorophyll comes out of the leaf. The alcohol is now green, and the leaf is white.

Put the leaf in a saucer so that it is flat. Flood it with iodine. See where you get a blue-black color indicating the presence of starch. The part that was covered by the cardboard remains white.

Plant leaves make food — sugars and starches — from water and carbon dioxide only in the presence of light. Remove the light and no food is made.

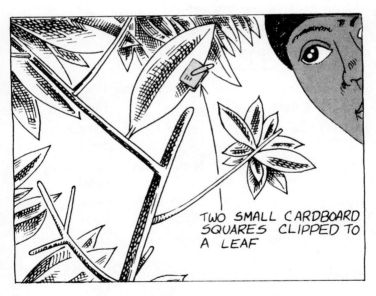

TWO SMALL CARDBOARD SQUARES CLIPPED TO A LEAF

Setup for "Photosynthesis" experiment.

137

Testing Fibers

Suppose you were a detective and you had a piece of fabric as a clue. Would you know what kind of fabric it was? Chemists can tell simply by burning it. The way a small sample of fabric burns and the kind of ash it forms are both good tests for identifying an unknown fiber.

CHECK WITH AN ADULT BEFORE YOU TRY THIS TEST. You will test fabric samples about ½ inch square. Hold your sample in a flame using metal tongs. Have a large foil ash tray or metal pan handy so you can put down your burning sample.

Compare your results with this table:

FIBER	FLAME	SMELLS LIKE	ASH
cotton	rapid, yellow	burning paper	fine, gray
linen	fairly fast	cotton	fine, gray
nylon	melts, no flame	celery	hard black bead
polyester	melts and burns	broiled fish	hard black bead
wool	slow, sizzling	burnt hair	hollow, fragile bead
silk	slow, small flame	burnt hair	shiny round bead
acetate	rapid, with sparks	vinegar	hard black bead

8. Chemistry Magic Tricks

Ever see a magic show when a magician made "wine" turn into "water"? You knew that it wasn't magic, but now you know it was chemistry. In this chapter, you will learn how to use chemistry to perform some magic tricks yourself. To get the effect, all it takes is some preparation. To be a compelling performer, you'll have to rehearse and get your "patter" down. Make up stories and jokes to tell as you perform the tricks. A good magic show is as much show business as it is special effects.

The tricks in this chapter work. But they may need some fine tuning to adjust to conditions in your "lab." That's part of the fun of being a chemist. I've put this chapter at the end of the book because an understanding of chemistry makes these tricks especially enjoyable.

One last reminder. Be sure and wash all glassware

thoroughly when you are finished to remove all traces
of chemicals that might be harmful.

The Water-to-Wine-to-Water Gambit

A solution goes from clear to red to clear. The explanation could be that "spirits" are trying to sabotage the
wine cellar so that the wine keeps disappearing.

MATERIALS AND EQUIPMENT

✗ two Ex-Lax tablets
hammer
small cup
measuring cup and spoons
✗ rubbing alcohol
spoon for stirring
pitcher
4 four-ounce glasses
white vinegar
§ ✗ ammonia

PREPARATION

Smash the Ex-Lax tablets with the hammer and put
them in the cup with two tablespoons of alcohol. Stir.
This is your phenolphthalein indicator, which will give
you the wine color.

Set up the pitcher and glasses as follows. Put ¼

teaspoon phenolphthalein in the first and third glass. (It is such a small amount that your audience will probably not notice it.) Put nothing in the second glass. Put ½ teaspoon vinegar in the fourth glass. Put 2 cups of water and ¼ teaspoon ammonia in the pitcher. DO NOT DRINK ANY OF THESE MIXTURES.

PERFORMANCE

Pour the water/ammonia mixture from the pitcher into all four glasses. The liquid in the first glass will be wine-colored, in the second, clear like water; in the third, wine-colored; and in the fourth, clear. Expressing surprise, pour the contents of the first three glasses back into the pitcher. The mixture will be wine-colored, even when you pour it back into the glasses. So now you have three out of four showing "wine." Pour the contents of all four glasses back into the pitcher. Presto! You've got "water," plain and simple. Even when you pour the liquid into the glasses "water" remains. Wash your glassware carefully after your performances.

The Chemistry Behind the Trick

Phenolphthalein in Ex-Lax is an acid-base indicator; it is colorless in acid, dark pink in base. Ammonia is a strong alkali and will produce the pink color in the indicator-doctored glasses. Vinegar is an acid that neutralizes the ammonia. When this happens, the indicator turns colorless, showing that the mixture is acidic.

Blush Test

Make the cheeks of a face in a drawing or photo turn red when asked an embarrassing question. You can have lots of fun with this one.

MATERIALS AND EQUIPMENT
✗ two Ex-Lax tablets
✗ two tablespoons rubbing alcohol
   small cup
   black-and-white drawing or photo of a face
   paintbrush
⧚ ✗ household ammonia

PREPARATION
Crush the Ex-Lax tablets and mix them with the alcohol to get a solution of phenolphthalein. Paint the cheeks of your portrait with this solution. Just before your performance, moisten the back of the portrait so that it is slightly damp.

PERFORMANCE
Hold the portrait up before your audience. Say that the person gets embarrassed easily and blushes if asked

the wrong question. Get members of the audience to ask questions. Sure enough, the cheeks turn red. The reason? You have secretly dipped in ammonia the index finger of the hand that is *not* holding the portrait. When you bring your finger near the portrait, the ammonia causes the phenolphthalein to indicate the presence of an alkali by turning red. You don't have to touch the picture. The fumes of the ammonia will do the job. Be sure to wash your hands when you're done.

Blush test.

The Chemistry Behind the Trick

The phenolphthalein is doing its thing as an indicator. The picture should be moist to ensure that the ammonia reacts with the indicator. The reason that the color fades is that ammonia evaporates very easily. It is called a *fugitive* substance because it disappears into the air. When it evaporates, the indicator returns to its original, colorless state.

Blue Again...and Again

Pour water into a glass and it changes into "ink." Pour the "ink" into another glass and it changes back into "water." Wave your wand and it's blue again.

MATERIALS AND EQUIPMENT
    1 tablespoon starch solution (see instructions below)
    3 clear colorless glasses
  ☠ ½ cup 3% hydrogen peroxide
    1/2 cup water
    1 tablespoon white vinegar
☠ ▲ a few drops iodine
  ☠ 1 or 2 drops hypo solution (mix 1 teaspoon hypo, from a photo store, in 1 tablespoon water)
    a wand

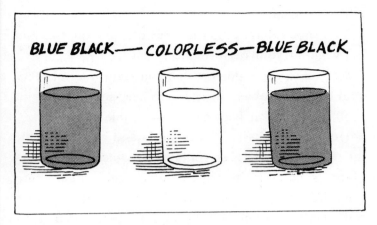

BLUE BLACK——COLORLESS—BLUE BLACK

A delayed reversible reaction.

PREPARATION

First, prepare the starch solution. Put one cup of water in a small saucepan. Add one teaspoon cornstarch. CHECK WITH AN ADULT BEFORE USING THE STOVE. Heat and stir until the cornstarch is completely dissolved. Add another cup of water. Store in a jar in the refrigerator. It will remain fresh for two or three days.

Put the starch solution, hydrogen peroxide, water and vinegar in one glass. It looks like water because the starch solution is so dilute that you can't detect the cloudiness. Put a few drops of iodine on the bottom of the second glass. (If the glass has a thick bottom, no one will notice the iodine.) Put 1 or 2 drops of hypo on the bottom of the third glass. DO NOT DRINK THESE MIXTURES.

You should have only the three prepared glasses and the wand at your performance.

Suggest to your audience that you know a secret agent who had the problem of trying to keep invisible ink invisible, but that it kept becoming visible again.

Hold up the glass of clear liquid and call it invisible ink. Pour it into the glass containing iodine. It turns blue-black. Then pour the contents of the second glass into the third glass, containing the hypo. Give the solution a stir with the wand. It will instantly become colorless again, but within 15 seconds it will change back to blue-black again. Wash your glassware carefully.

The Chemistry Behind the Trick

When you pour the first glass into the second glass, the iodine reacts with the starch to give the typical blue-black color that is a test for starch. When you pour the starch-iodine compound into the hypo, the hypo forms a colorless compound with the iodine, freeing the starch, which is also colorless; so the blue-black color disappears.

Meanwhile, a fourth substance, hydrogen peroxide, is slowly breaking down and adding oxygen to the mixture. Oxygen forms a more permanent compound with the hypo than the iodine; so the hypo leaves the iodine and combines with the oxygen. This now frees the iodine to recombine with the starch. Presto! Blue-black time again. Since it takes time for enough oxygen to evolve to make this happen, there is a delayed return to the "ink" stage. It happens without you doing a thing.

You can get the reaction to reverse itself again by delivering more hypo to the system. One way of doing this is to use ordinary paper glue or paste or rubber cement to glue a few crystals of hypo to one end of your wand. Use this end to stir the mixture after its second blue-black stage, until the color disappears. And again, if you wait, the blue color may reappear by itself.

This trick takes some fiddling with to get the measurements exactly right. But that's where the fun is!

A Clear Shake

You can make a bottle of root-beer-colored liquid turn to clear water by giving it a few shakes.

MATERIALS AND EQUIPMENT
ϟ hypo crystals
  rubber cement
  small bottle with cap
  water
ϟ ▲ iodine

Glue a few crystals of hypo to the inside of the bottle cap with the rubber cement. Pour water into the bottle and add a few drops of iodine to give it the right color.

To make the change happen, simply shake the bottle so that the hypo goes into solution. DO NOT DRINK THIS MIXTURE. Wash your glassware promptly.

The Chemistry Behind the Trick

Hypo (sodium thiosulfate) reacts with iodine to form a colorless compound.

Thought Waves for Milk

You ask your audience to think about milk as you pour "water" into a glass. Lo and behold, "milk" turns up in the glass. This trick shows the power of positive thinking!

MATERIALS AND EQUIPMENT

▲ ✗ household bleach containing *sodium hypochlorite* (read the label carefully)

glass tumbler

✗ hypo solution (1/2 cup hypo in 2 cups water)

glass pitcher

wand to serve as stirring rod

148

Put a few drops of bleach on the bottom of the glass so that no one can notice that it's there. Put the hypo solution in the pitcher. You should bring out only the pitcher, the glass and the wand for your performance.

CAUTION: DO NOT UNDER ANY CIRCUM-STANCES ALLOW ANYONE TO DRINK THIS SO-LUTION; IT'S POISONOUS.

PERFORMANCE

Tell your audience that you have a pitcher of "water." Ask them to name other drinks. Usually someone will say "milk." But if that doesn't happen, you might bring up the name by suggesting that there is a perfect food that is drinkable.

Then ask everyone to think hard about milk (or to chant "milk" aloud over and over again) while you pour the "water" into the glass. Use the wand to stir. In a short period of time (depending on the strength of the hypo solution) "skim milk" will appear in the glass. Since it has a watery appearance, you might point out that you've made skim milk because according to some doctors it is more healthful than whole milk.

Remove and carefully wash the glass after the trick is finished, since the white precipitate will settle out.

The Chemistry Behind the Trick

Sodium thiosulfate reacts with sodium hypochlorite to form a precipitate of the element sulfur. This finely divided form of sulfur is called *milk of sulfur* because of its white appearance.

A Final Word

For the most part, the chemistry you have explored in this book deals with the simplest of compounds and could be done successfully without careful measurement of quantities. You have barely scratched the surface of a science that has transformed the world in fields such as medicine, engineering, electronics and fashion. Through chemistry we are beginning to understand cancer and heart disease, the very secrets of life. Understanding matter on its molecular level enables us to do things that we couldn't do before. We can make fabric from coal, fuel from garbage, aspirin from powdered starch and countless other substances. We have not yet made gold from less precious metals, but modern chemistry would no doubt dazzle the alchemists: it's magic beyond their wildest dreams.

Chemistry is a well-established science. But it is only just beginning to make its contribution to the world.

INDEX

Page numbers in *italics* refer to illustrations.

151